A DUBROVNIK WAR STORY
THEY WON'T HURT ME, MOM!

Anita Rakidžija

CIP-Katalogizacija u publikaciji
Znanstvena knjižnica Dubrovnik

UDK 821.163.42-3

RAKIDŽIJA, Anita
   A Dubrovnik war story : they won't hurt me, mom! / Anita
Rakidžija ;<photographs Miro Kerner, Pavo Urban ; Enlarged
ed. - Dubrovnik : The Croatian associationa of civilian victims
of the War for freedom at the Dubrovnik-Neretva county, 2009
135 str. : ilustr. (djelomice u bojama) ; 21 cm
   Prijevod djela: Neće oni mene, mama!.

ISBN 978-953-95186-0-4

490624063

Vlaho Rakidžija, 2ⁿᵈ February 1983. - 30ᵗʰ August 1992.

Old Harbour in flames on St. Nicholas' Day, 1991. (photo: Miro Kerner)

photo: Miro Kerner

photo: Miro Kerner

6

photo: Miro Kerner

photo: Miro Kerner

7

photo: Miro Kerner

photo: Miro Kerner

photo: Miro Kerner

photo: Miro Kerner

11

The monument dedicated to the memory of Vlaho and Ivo

13

archive: Dubrovacki vijesnik

archive: Dubrovacki vijesnik

14

archive: Dubrovacki vijesnik

archive: Dubrovacki vijesnik

archive: Dubrovacki vijesnik

archive: Dubrovacki vijesnik

17

archive: Slobodna dalmacija

archive: Slobodna dalmacija

archive: Slobodna dalmacija

archive: Slobodna dalmacija

archive: Slobodna dalmacija

Preface by the translator:

One of Dubrovnik's celebrated poets had once written: "War is the death of the nature of man." The war which was forced upon Dubrovnik and its surrounding area in the autumn of 1991 was a bloody episode which has brought mayhem and destruction. It has threatened, and in many cases succeeded, to kill all that is honest and good in people, to kill the very nature of man. It has left every man, woman and, indeed, a child with a war story. Each is special and none two are alike.

Mrs. Rakidžija's book is a war story. The translator of this book has dealt, over the past years, with several books having to do with war. Most of them, especially if they contain an element of personal tragedy, are marked by a specific bitterness. The book in your hands, even though it has that specific element, is not bitter at all. The author is honest; she does not add things to the truth, nor does she omit them to make facts more pleasant. Her style very fresh, documentary to a point of not being impersonal, could be described as almost journalistic.

This book does not offer any answers. It does not offer an absolute, infallible account; it is not THE story, it is A story. It does, however, offer a unique window into the lives of ordinary people, the ones whose lives are usually most viciously affected and changed by the atrocities of war. These are the people whose stories are not found in history books; they are not "important" enough for their stories to be noted. But they are the ones who are the easiest to understand. They are the ones who survived. Their voices have to be heard.

M.S.

Cars burning, Nov. 1991. (photo: Pavo Urban)

Croatia – summer of 1991.

The Yugoslav Army has been attacking the Northeast of Croatia. Small places are being swallowed as they approach Vukovar. Great big lines of agonized and scared people are leaving their homes. Roadblocks and unrest are also taking their toll in the area around Knin.

Nobody is able to look at what tomorrow is going to bring without feeling anxious. We are very worried as we watch this news on the TV. We live in the Southeast of Croatia. Dubrovnik shares a border with the enemy who has earnestly attempted to disarm the city. Weapons intended for the Civil Guard have been deliberately taken and steered towards the near by town of Trebinje. We are scared because the future is uncertain for us. Women and children from Vukovar and the surrounding area arrive in Dubrovnik seeking refuge and temporary accommodation in hotels and private boarding houses. We are all worried. A helping hand is expected from the world, but no reaction is forthcoming.

I go to work to Dubrovnik every day. We hear news of heavily armed troops gathering at Ivanica, just above the city. Ivanica represents Dubrovnik's Northeast border, that is, the border between the Republic of Croatia and Bosnia and Herzegovina. People living in these areas, who work in Dubrovnik, leave every weekend, lately even daily, for Trebinje and Bileća. Many of them have not been to work for a couple of days, offering excuses that either they, or their parents, are ill. With each passing day, our doubts are greater. We fear the worst. The flames of war are blazing up furiously in the Northeastern regions of Croatia. We are stockpiling food for the worst case scenario. Flour and sugar are among the most important items. By the end of September the Yugoslav Army battle ships are imposing a sea blockade around Dubrovnik. We have been warned to be cautious of lights in our hoses and on the terraces at night. Fear slowly begins to creep in our bones. I do the supper dishes in almost complete darkness. Our kitchen window faces the sea where the gloomy shapes of gunboats can be seen. I keep the candle next to my feet, away from the heavily draped window. No light is supposed to be seen from the outside.

Men are keeping watch just above the village at night. My husband leaves with them every night. They are armed mostly with hunting rifles. I stay home alone, with my children and my mother in law to keep me company. The fear that I feel prevents me from resting. The older people are spreading gruesome tales from the "last" (Second World) War. In the morning my husband returns and I have to leave for work, tired and scared. This goes on for several days. The unwholesomeness of the atmosphere gives me the chills. I lock all the doors at night, checking, and often double-checking, to be certain that they are indeed locked. I jump at every little noise as I wait for the morning.

Orašac, 1ˢᵗ October 1991.

I got up at about 6:30 to go to work. As I opened the window I enjoyed a moment of the beautiful early autumn morning. Suddenly, an unknown sound draws my attention. Hollow sounds of detonations echoing from somewhere near by. Too near! The chills are here again. Could it be that something horrible is starting to take place in Dubrovnik, the city which we all thought was so safe. The Radio reports: "We are under attack! The enemy has shelled targets in Komolac..." We were left in the dark; the electricity was cut. The fear is starting to take physical shape. I hurry, pull my children out of their beds and quickly take them to the "new house". The "new house" has two concrete floors; I feel it is safe, as I shove them into the pantry under the stairs. The city is under general alarm – I hear the eerie sound of alarm for the very first time – and I feel, anticipate, the horror of war that has come to knock on our doors too. Several days ago we have all received our shelter assignments for the case of the emergency. Our neighbor is running around in panic, saying: "Everybody, go to the shelter, everybody to the main shelter. These are the orders of the Civil Guard." I grab my children by their hands, feeling the blood pumping in my ears ever so slowly, as my heart begins to pound. The shelter is only a 100 or so yards away, but it is so far at this moment. Vlaho is big, eight and a half, and he walks in front of me as I lead Ivana, his five-years-old sister by the hand, carrying in my other hand few of the things I have prepared for the case of the attack. We race across, under the olive trees, wondering – when will we arrive...! My son is not afraid, only his mother and sister are. At last, we make it. The house that has been designated as a shelter is already filled with women, the elderly and children. I seek out for a piece of floor that looks safer and place my children there. The building has four, maybe five floors –concrete slates – and it is supposed to be safe in the case of an air raid. Fear colors the faces of people, and many are panicking, saying that the Yugoslav Army is very near, that there is no way out. I am scared; I am particularly scared for the children. The smaller children are crying. There is no water, electricity either. My mother-in-law is brave – she stays behind to make a meal. I dare to take a shortcut home, in a hurry, to take some food for the children and I rush back to the shelter. The darkness is approaching slowly, our first night of uncertainty; the first night of war in this area. We all sleep fully dressed and with our shoes on. We are ordered to keep the noise down and not to use the flash-lights because the building is located on top of a small hill, facing the sea. The three gunboats are lurking in the dark waters. Someone has a battery operated radio, and the news is listened to in pious silence. What shall we hear? Nothing good, I expect. The night is long, frightfully long; smaller children are often crying and the older women cannot sleep, so they talk. There are no beds or cots – some old blankets are the only thing between us and the cold floor tiles. The children have finally gone to sleep.

Five in the morning, I start hearing voices, people talking. Everyone is awake, the children too, of course, it is time for the news again – time for panic, fear and a plethora of wrong information. I clasp the rosary beads in my pocket; dear God, please keep us safe. With sunrise things appear a bit less hard. I think: "Well, the first war night is behind us…what now?"

Next day, in a brief period of silence between the detonations, I decide to take the children home. Once again I shove them into the corner of the new house; the corner which we felt was the safest place to be. My husband returns from his watch duty to check on us, stays with us for an hour or two and then leaves again. The afternoon is approaching and we all head back to the shelter. We are the wiser now; the tiles were so cold last night, so we haul some old mattresses with us, and I take some sweaters and long slacks for the children. Another difficult night, news, nothing good. The planes are bombing a nearby village of Osojnik, flying over us, turning over the island of Kalamota and returning to attack the Croatian Army, the brave men defending their homes. Once again, I manage to collect myself, and we go home to eat something before heading back to the shelter. The Civil Guard demands discipline. We are ordered to stay together at all times, in case we have to be evacuated.

4ᵗʰ October – The evacuation of women and children to the city proper is already being considered. The motorway is blocked; the village of Komolac is being bombed heavily, as well as the gas reservoirs at Sustjepan, the sea is controlled by gunboats. There seems to be almost no way out. Panic is growing by the minute. The night is approaching – each one more difficult and filled with panic than the last one. A strong northern wind starts to blow, almost shaking the house, bringing all sorts of sounds to us. Children have mostly gone to sleep; the grown-ups are not able to. Some of the women are saying that the trucks are near-by, that we are doomed. I hate the shelter; I resent this multitude of people because they only add to my fear. Another dawn breaks, bringing relief with the light. We are all still alive, there are no trucks, nor the Yugoslav Army, and we are grateful for this. Each night the women pray, reciting the rosary in the darkness.

5th October – More plans about the evacuation of women and children. I go home with my children. My mother-in-law leads the way; she does not seem to be afraid. The dull hum of the helicopter is heard right behind the nearby hill. She walks on bravely with Vlaho right behind her. I shout for him to stop, but he answers: "They won't hurt me, Mommy!" and continues on. I take Ivana by the hand and take cover under the branches of an olive tree. My heart aches as I hear her say: "Dear Lord, please save us!", and I attempt to console her, but I too am very afraid. As the sound of the helicopter fades away in the distance, we finally reach the house. The children are placed in the make-shift shelter and I bring them some warm milk, not allowing them to leave their little corner. Vlaho complains, he would like to leave, but it is out of the question.

I make lunch, a more lavish one than usual. The electricity is still out and I am aware that the meat and vegetable supplies from the freezer will not keep for much longer. After lunch it is back to the shelter which is, by this time, taken over by fear. The decision is made – women and children must leave Orašac. The grenades have started a forest fire which is spreading rapidly towards us. Some of the women have decided to leave. I am still not sure of anything; my mind seems to have slipped into a lower gear. I ask the Civil Guard officials: "How do you plan to transport us to the city, by which route? Roads are closed, the sea routes are blocked." They are silent.

We leave the shelter and I take my children home again. At about four in the afternoon my husband comes, running toward me and shouting: "You and the kids are leaving for the city right now!" I cannot feel my arms or legs. I answer: "I don't want to, Tonći. I am scared." "You have to leave, and it has to be right away, urgently. Fishing boats are leaving from Zaton, so take the kids and go." My eyes begin to fill with tears as I run to get some underwear and a few trinkets. I also take an old blanket, a plastic container with about a gallon of water, as I know that there is no drinking water in the city either, some milk and some instant cocoa-drink powder. In the confusion I forget that I am wearing my husband's pants, as they were more appropriate for the shelter. It is still quite warm, Indian summer, so I do not bother to pack any winter clothes. This will all be over in a couple of days anyway, I think.

My husband urges his mother to go with us, but she refuses. We say our goodbyes hastily. Vlaho helps me carry the things; we hop in the car and head towards Zaton. Arriving at the nick of time we run toward the boat that has slowly began to leave the pier. Local people are mad that the women and children from Orašac are using their transport, but they still take us on board. Everything is done in great haste, we get in the boat and I wrap the blanket around my children. With tears in my eyes, I wave a goodbye to my husband, the children blow kisses to their father. The boat takes off to uncertainty as we watch the hills above Zaton ablaze.

The boat that we have boarded does not take us straight to Babin Kuk. We are ordered to disembark at the Zaton cape and wait for another boat. We stand on the pier, about twenty of us, women and children, awaiting salvation. The boat arrives. Somebody takes Ivana and shoves her into the boat, while the frightened child yells and shouts. Children are boarded first. The inside of the boat is pitch-black.

Ivana is stiff with fear; I shout: "You'll trample the child!" She is almost paralyzed with panic as the people are boarding uncontrollably, stepping over one another. My turn finally comes. My son is dignified and silent; I admire his obvious lack of fear. He helps me with the things. I ask some of the older children to pass Ivana to me, since she cannot stop crying. When I finally get a hold of my little girl I take her firmly by the hand. "Don't be scared, baby", I tell her, "Mommy is here." The boat engine starts to hum rhythmically and we start the second stage of our sea voyage, sailing very close to the shore line. I feel my whole body cramping and my throat is clenched with fear. My mind races with dark possibilities: "What if we are hit? What if we stumble upon a sea mine?" Ivana cries incessantly, I whisper into her ear, attempting to break the fear without showing just how scared I myself am. Vlaho sits in silence. We sit on top of the M-48 guns. The man who navigates the boat and the woman, whose head occasionally pops out, inform us of our position. We are heading along the shore line. Fearful detonations resound, and my fear grows. What if we get hit?

The engine noise is loud so we do not know what is happening in the outside world. They tell us: "We are turning towards Babin Kuk." We are upon the open sea. It has been perhaps twenty minutes, but it seems that we have been sailing for hours. "Are we ever going to arrive?", I wonder. The engines are tuning down. The man at the mast shouts: "Babin Kuk! We have arrived!" The spasm in my body seems to subside; I suddenly feel that we are saved. The Civil Guard officials await us at the hotel "Minčeta" pier. Unaware of anything, I disembark, guarding the most prized possession of them all - a gallon canister of drinking water. Vlaho helps me carry our things, the two or three plastic bags of possessions, and the water. Ivana is already being carried by the hand, and I yell: "No, wait! She's going to be shocked without me!" I have no clue as to where we are all going. We arrive in the front of the hotel at five-thirty in the afternoon. The night is nigh, - the hotel is full; a great commotion arises. Many people know where they are going – some have a brother, some a sister, some own an apartment in the city. My children and I, we have nothing. All I know is that, at parting, my husband told us "Get in touch with my uncle." It took about fifteen minutes for the ruckus to clear up. At that moment, we heard the sirens – the general alarm siren is sounded. We start running toward the hotel. We are told that the ground floor corridors are the shelter. I push my children in front of me as I carry the luggage. The corridors are completely dark. We arrive to the so-called shelter – the dark corridor. A candle is burning in the flower pot.

There are a lot of people I do not know. My neighbor is there with her children. We are scuffled in a corner, sitting silently. There is no water, no power, the toilets are all locked. The children are hungry. All I have are some dry biscuits and a little water, but I do not give it to them. They get sleepy. At about eight-thirty in the evening I take some chairs from the restaurant, put two and two together, making it possible for them to lie down. There is no blanket or pillow, but they say nothing. My neighbor's brother picks her up and I am left all alone among so many strangers. They ask me where I am from. "From Orašac.", I respond shortly. I look at my children, barely holding back the tears. For the first time in their lives they sleep sitting, their arms and legs dangling from the chairs. I ask a woman, an acquaintance of mine, to watch them, as I walk through the darkness of the reception hall. I ask for a blanket to cover my children. I am told that there are none, but a young man takes pity on us and manages to bring us two blankets. Truly grateful, I descend into the dark corridor and cover my children to protect them from the cold. Hours rush by, soon it is eleven. People start to stir; all of them have already been assigned rooms. Not us. Those more courageous are leaving shelters and going to their rooms. It is still outside, nothing can be heard. Around midnight almost everybody has left the shelter/corridor. A woman I know, having recognized us, decides to take us into her room for the night. I tell her not to worry about us and ask her if she could bring us a candle, since the one that is burning is almost spent.

I head to the restaurant, which is right along the hallway.

Through the large terrace doors I see Orašac and Zaton, with the great fire behind. Everything seems to be burning. I worry about my husband and his mother. Marija, the woman who has offered to take us into her room, has figured out a way for us to fit into the hotel room. Worn out, I accept the kind offer. I take my sleeping daughter in my arms and I slowly lift my son, lean him against my side and half drag him behind me. We climb a dark flight of stairs and then start along an equally dark hallway. Somehow I manage to get them to that blessed room. Marija turns the flashlight on for me to see. Extremely tired as they are, the children just throw themselves on the bed. I take their shoes off and cover them with a blanket. "For the first time since you were born,", I think to myself, "you have not eaten for over twelve hours."

I sleep for awhile. The dawn wakes me, heavy and gloomy. I get up early and ask Marija whether I could heat some milk somewhere. The answer is negative. I feel a stab to my heart; is it possible that my children will have to go without breakfast, too? They wake up as well. Ever since the war began, they get up very early. I ask them to wait for me and run to the front desk. I need to call my husband's uncle before he leaves to work. There is a long line, and there is nothing I can do except wait patiently. I have called him the night before, but could not get through. Ploče, the part of the city where he lives, was under attack from the gunboats. Finally, I get my turn on the phone, and he answers. With tears in my voice, I beg him to help us. "We do not have a room, I can't make breakfast and my kids are hungry and thirsty." He is willing to find me a room in one of the hotels, but he can also come and take me to his place if I want him to. I decide to go to his house, as my husband has suggested. I get the children dressed and take them, hungry and cranky, in front of the hotel. Uncle arrives and I start crying; for the first time in my life I feel overwhelmed. "Don't cry,", he says, "let's go!". We take those few belongings that we have and follow him to the car.

On 6th October at 7:30 AM we get to his house. It seems quite safe, with three thick concrete slabs and a roof. I presumed they were alone in it. I enter a studio apartment which faces west, towards the Old Town. To my great surprise, some people, unknown to me, are also there. Friends of the family from Župa Dubrovačka. They have fled their home some time ago and have been offered sanctuary here. I feel very uncomfortable in these awkward new circumstances. For the first time I notice that I am still wearing my husband's old slacks, and very old shoes, accompanied by a matching shirt. Unable to think clearly in the panic, I have taken very little clothes, so I barely have anything. I am relieved to find that uncle's family has a gas cooker, so the milk is promptly heated for the children. Thank God that I am at least able to give something warm to my babies.

We eat lunch, getting to know each other as we begin our refugee life together under somebody else's roof. I still hope that this will all be over soon and that we will be going home in a few days. These thoughts calm me down a bit. The phone lines to Orašac are dead. We are completely cut from our home and from our family. Night approaches, we have to make some sort of sleeping arrangement. Uncle tells us that the room we are in is the safest, so we all sleep in it – some on the floor, some in beds. Children are pretty confused. Nine of us sleep in the same room that night. I wake to the first dawn in a strange house, feeling uncomfortable. Refrigerators do not work since there is no power, so our milk has gone sour. Uncle offers me some powdered milk, and I am very grateful for it. Not being the one to sit and do nothing, I help with the cooking and cleaning. The children are silent; there is nothing for them to do and everything is strange and new to them. Ivana has a Barbie doll, Vlaho an old toy car. The level of panic is growing in the city because of the severe shortage of drinking water. Our host makes at times heroic efforts to get food and water for us all. There is a lot of us, no water for the toilet. Hygiene is down to a minimum. I think to myself: "Can it be that this is Dubrovnik, that we are reduced to this?" Often do my thoughts go to our house; there is water in the well and food stocked for winter. It is difficult to get anything here; vegetable is nowhere to be found. But the lack of water is hardest to bear. Night comes early and the days are really tough. At night we watch some strange signals from under mount Srđ. They make us shiver. What is being told, and by whom? Uncle goes to work each day, we stay behind and, seemingly, await doom.

Radio program is reduced to news on the hour. Reports are not very good. The "civilized" world has turned a deaf ear on our toil. It is nice there, in the West, they have not felt a longing for a glass of cold water. After all, what are we to them? I catch myself thinking of my family. My parents are in the "Adriatic" hotel. They were evacuated by buses on the very first day of war. I have called them to let them know where I was. My sister lives in Duba. I have talked to her on 1st October, and the lines have been dead since. Ivana keeps asking about her Daddy, when is he coming to get us. "Soon, baby.", I try to console her, not knowing if we are ever going to see him myself.

A monotonous and painful week has passed since or family was broken up for the first time. On the seventh day, at 9 AM, there is a knock on the door. My husband! I jump and get to him faster than I ever thought I could. Tears stream down my cheeks; he is barely holding his while he hugs the children and showers them with kisses. How did he get here, I ask him. He does not answer. He has brought us four gallons of water and some food (fruit, vegetables, some eggs and milk), all luxury items at the time. I am extremely sorry to find out that he cannot stay for more than half an hour; the neighbor is waiting for him. A great stone is sitting on my chest, but he has to go. He is a Croatian soldier now. He kisses the children goodbye and I follow him half way down the street. "Take care of yourself," he tells me, "and please take care of our children."

"Of course I will, don't worry. And you take special care of yourself.", I answer and the tears appear again. I watch him leave; he turns and shouts at me: "I'll come again if I can. If anything happens, I'll be coming to stay with you." I return, mixed feelings in my heart; I am really happy that he came, but I am so sad that he has to leave. I was also worried about him crossing the wooden draw bridge into the Old City since I knew it was damaged by grenades and watched by the enemy. As I enter the house I am forced to answer the children's: "Where did Daddy go? When is he coming back?" and it takes my mind of the more serious issues.

My son is quite ill by this time and I also have a rather severe cold. I am guessing that we have the sea breeze on the boat to thank for this. Vlaho is running a high fever, so I go to the infirmary to get some medicine. I also started sick days as far as work is concerned. There is no power, anyway, so the computers do not work. My work, data processing, is out of the question.

I worry about my son; he is burning up in fever and eats very little. I go to the Old Town and go from one shop to the other looking for some marmalade, butter, any sort of spread. Sales clerks find it very amusing that I would even ask. The stores now hold only some liquor, bread, noodles and rice. That is it.

In a couple of days Vlaho is feeling better. However, since trouble never comes alone, everyone in the house has gotten head-lice. I am appalled, having never even seen them before. I ask my husband's brother-in-law to get us some lice powder. He promises to try, since that is also one of the items in shortage. I am amazed that even that can't be found, but considering the much lowered standard of hygiene, I guess that many people in Dubrovnik have gotten lice. Finally, a box of lice powder is obtained. I powder the children's heads with it. The next day I am supposed to wash their hair. It is cloudy and rains at times. How am I to wash their hair and, above all, how should I dry it? I feel miserable.

Suddenly, we hear the airplanes and we all run to the shelter.

Powerful explosions resound. After awhile the grown-ups go to the front door. The slopes of the hill are burning above us. It is dusk and the fire is spreading, swallowing everything that comes in its path. Voices are heard as more and more people join in to put the fire out. "There is no water!" shouts are heard, "Why is there no water?". The day slowly fades away into darkness. We are all scared and exhausted.

In the evening of 20th October we watch as rockets are being fired from gunboats at Kupari. It is dark enough to see the multi-colored flares of missiles flying toward the village. We are scared; Vlaho wants to see what is happening, but I do not let him. He complains, saying: "Mom, do you seriously think that they're going to fire at me?" Still, I do not give in to his wishes. The next day is quite. It is also sunny, so I decide to wash their hairs, as they will be able to dry it in the sun.

I never knew how difficult it is to get rid of head lice. The process has to be repeated several times. We sleep with our heads wrapped in white scarves, the hair full of the smelly powder. I feel pathetic, miserable and forgotten.

The Radio is our only companion, our link with the world. "This is Radio Dubrovnik with news from our war studio. The war is gaining momentum, Župa Dubrovačka is under attack, the villages of Brgat and Osojnik. Nine people have lost their lives in Mokošica." We feel awful and I start to loose hope of returning home soon. The names of the killed people are read. I know some of them.

During the intermissions between attacks Vlaho always wants to do something. There is a swimming pool in the yard and he has taken it upon himself to sweep it and gather up dried leaves. I let him do it, because the pool is in a shielded area of the yard facing west. He always liked to do something to help when we were home. I understand that he is bored here, so I allow this "pastime".

The next days the clouds gather. Our host has an idea – we could collect water in the swimming pool by way of fire hoses which would conduct the rain from the roof. Vlaho is thrilled to be of use as he helps unroll the heavy hoses. Soon it starts to rain. We hear the water running into the pool. Every once in a while someone runs to the pool to see how much water has gathered. We are so happy. Some of the water is filtered through gauze and set aside for drink water. Neighbors put buckets under the drains or collect water right from the pavement. We are glad as little children – now we have the water to wash ourselves and to flush the toilet. We are even able to wash our clothes, heating the water on open fire in the garden. Even though it can at times get strenuous living here I feel privileged as I compare my situation to those of the people living in hotels.

Many are already leaving Dubrovnik by boat – the only way out of, or into, the besieged city. I stay. As long as my husband stays here, so will we, and I know that he has no intention of leaving. My thoughts go to him once again. I try to find something out from some people who have their own radio transceiver set, but am told that there is no contact with Orašac. The feelings of sadness and melancholy weigh heavily on my heart. Living gets more difficult every day. Winter is approaching and we are so poorly clothed. The phones are dead, so there is no way for me to get in touch with my husband. Suddenly, around 20th October, he appears out of the blue. His presence seems to lift some of the heaviness from the whole situation. He has brought us some clothes, nothing, however, for the winter. I ask him why he had not brought us overcoats or winter jackets. "This has to be over soon," he answers, "you'll be home in a little while." His hope affects me, I start hoping too. In vain. The phone keeps ringing; family and friends call to check up on us.

Our host has sent his two daughters to Split to stay with his brother. The crowded house is a bit less crowded now. The ship they are on is ordered to turn toward the Montenegrin port of Zelenika. This is the first time this has happened. Panic creeps into the house. Aunt and uncle are shocked, they cry – their children are on board. I try to say something to make things easier, but the situation is very tense. We eagerly await the news. Everything is resolved to our satisfaction by morning. The ship underwent an inspection and then it continued on its way to Split. Sense of relief is almost tangible. From that day each ship that sails from Dubrovnik has to go to Zelenika to be inspected before it is allowed to go to its intended destination.

People begin to panic. Women and children are leaving the city in great numbers. Heavy artillery is now aimed at residential areas. Alarms are frequent, general alarm the most. The grip is tightening on the overcrowded, tormented city. The only thing the citizens are expecting these days is the news, which lasts for three, maybe five minutes. Disappointment lasts until the next news brings us a new one.

By the end of October humanitarian aid starts arriving. Local authorities are making lists of residents and refugees. Rations are being distributed once a week in the beginning. The lines are immensely long and it is tiring to wait in front of the garage where the Local Authority of the City Subdistrict of Ploče has set up headquarters. Fear has a hold on people waiting in lines. People queue in open air, in plain view for the enemy. People wait in line patiently, even when it starts to rain, feeling utterly humiliated inside, but we have no choice. A world renown city, most of whose inhabitants used to be pretty well of, is reduced to poverty. All that the West is doing for us is humanitarian aid. Many of the food and medical supplies we have received are long expired. However, as they say, beggars can't be choosers, and we are grateful and make use of everything. We vainly hope that our cause for freedom will be helped, but the "world" has turned a deaf ear.

As time goes by, it gets colder by the day. I look for trousers or some pantyhose for my children, anything to keep them warm. All the stores have the same answer: "Regretfully, our stock is gone. We have nothing." With tears in my eyes, I continue my quest. At last, to my relief, I manage to find two pairs of underwear and shoes for my son.

Having exhausted all other options, I call a good friend of mine from work and I ask for help. "My kids are cold," I tell her, "there's nothing in the stores. Could you please spare some clothes? Anything will do." Right away she sends over some warm clothes and a pair of shoes for Ivana. She also remembers me and sends me some winter clothes too. I will be grateful to her as long as I live.

My husband's sister phones me these days. They found refuge in Montovjerna, a city quarter where it is quite dangerous. Her family is leaving for Rijeka, since they are cramped in a small apartment with a lot of other people. She asks me if perhaps I would like to go with her.

Once again, I refuse to even consider it. I am not going anywhere until I have talked to my husband.

My father calls right after that and tells me that my sister has left for Rijeka, too. I burst into tears I cannot control. I realize it is better for her to go; she is pregnant, due in two months. I don't know why I cry, but I guess it was the proverbial one drop too many. It is so difficult. My husband does not come any more, I know nothing of him. The radio only reports of the events in the eastern part of the area around Dubrovnik and in the village and high-rise estate of Mokošica. No information is offered for the villages west of the city, so we are in the dark. The sirens go on very often., the Yugoslav Army is not very selective about its targets. Grenades are falling all over the city. I shove my children into the safest corner of the room and do not let them walk even around the room, even though the whole room is perfectly safe. The window is closed all the time, protected by some old mattresses we have stacked in front of it. It is very dark at all times inside, since the room is partly under the ground. Our life is candle lit. We are all pale by now from spending all that time in the dark; we resemble miners. The fear grows daily. Croatian Army is not able to hold its positions. Should that surprise us? Croatians have withstood, against all odds, a superiorly armed enemy for too long. The enemy we used to call our very own National Army is armed by the weaponry bought from the federal budget, to which Croatia has contributed for forty five years. The irony is lost on us at the time. The favorite target of choice for gunboats and airplanes is our stronghold at mount Srđ, an old Napoleonic fortress. A handful of brave boys is not giving in.

October is drawing to its end. My birthday, by far the hardest one in my life, has passed. It is marked by my family being broken, uncertainty, fear and the longing for my home. I hide my tears, so that nobody can see them. My birthday wish was for all this to be over, preferably with a happy ending. Occasionally, when the sounds of artillery stop, I let the children take a breath of fresh air at the door, but only for a couple of minutes at a time. As planes suddenly appear, I shout, nearly scream, at them to get in. My daughter asks me later on: "Mommy, how come we never had to hide when the planes would fly over our house?"

Vlaho is full of life and always eager to help. He fills the containers with water from the pool. Of course, as soon as I hear the already familiar sound of grenades either flying over us, or detonating, I do not allow him to go out. I get angry with him because he is hauling four gallon containers. "That's heavy for you, son.", I try to tell him, but he just waves me off: "Don't worry, Mommy, I can handle it."

Children are very bored, but they try to find things to do. Ivana plays with her doll and Vlaho ties a piece of wood on a rope and lugs it around in the swimming pool, pretending it is a Croatian battle ship coming to our rescue. I do not let them go very far from the front door to our apartment. The house has a large yard, but it is too dangerous to go to its eastern side. The Yugoslav flag is waving over cannon barrels at a panoramic rest stop right above us, to the east.

28th October – We can see them, and they can see us. The nights are hellish; the enemy is expected to attempt a breakthrough into the city any night now. Our batteries are gone, so we are not able to even listen to the news any more. The older son of our co-habitants, the family from Župa, manages to get his hands on a car battery, and the radio is hooked to it. We are glad to hear the news, such as it is, again. Every dawn brings solace; one more anxiety-filled night is behind us. Uncle works at Babin Kuk, cooking for the refugees in one of the hotels. His work is very strenuous – there is not nearly enough water, and they are running out of gas. He is always in a bad mood when he gets home, so the rest of us are mostly silent, not wishing to contribute to the already tense situation. The children sit in the corner and nobody says a word for hours. He is upset by the radio, by the news and by this whole situation. Frankly, none of us sees a way out of it; we are all home sick, but to no avail.

Hotels filled with refugees are also frequently targeted by the enemy. There are more civilian casualties daily, many of them refuges who have fled their homes in order to save their lives. Another night falls; we go to bed early, mostly to save candles, since we are running out. Running out of anything, matches, candles, batteries, means a long wait in a dangerous line. Sometimes, like with candles, there are simply none to be bought. Many have remembered to buy candles in churches, but that source has fast dried out. We go to bed around six; nights are too long, so we talk in the dark.

Seven of us are sleeping in one room; some have beds, those less lucky sleep on the floor. During the attacks this is a multi-purpose room; sleeping-sitting-smoking-dining room. While we lie in the dark, talking, suddenly a bright, flickering light shines through our window. The very thought that the enemies have descended from the hill and are shining flashlights around the house drives me insane. "We're doomed!", I think to myself, "My poor children!" I try to think of a place to hide them in. Each second as long as a year, the light still shines and then goes out. Everyone is silent. Somebody whispers, barely audibly: "What is this?" More silence. We expect the soldiers to burst in, crushing through the door. Nothing happens. Fear makes us all need to use the restroom. Tiptoeing through the dark, feeling ones way down the wall, it is not easy. Someone manages to gather some bravery and the door is slowly opened. Nobody is there.

In the morning we find out that the strange lights were flare rockets. The day is tense, as usual. We cook, preparing food for a few days. In the absence of a fridge, which is, of course, no use without electricity, we keep our food outside. It is hung on the branches of an orange tree growing in front of the door. Sometimes stray cats manage to get to our food and eat it. The food manages to keep for rather some time, even though it is still quite warm. Whatever goes bad is buried in the back yard. The yard is a blessing in the prevention of certain diseases. Everything that could possibly cause harm is buried.

One day fire trucks start filling up an old well near our house. The line is long for a four gallon ration. It is possible that the water would be gone by the time our turn comes.

We are constantly within the firing range of snipers, since they are all of them positioned in the hills above us. Gunfire could also be heard from some of the houses after dark. Dubrovnik is basically on the palm of their hand. We have learned to stick close to walls and move by the side alleys if we must go to the town to buy something. This usually means medicine, since there is nothing else. The city seems to have run out of everything, and the medical supplies are also almost spent.

Lice, which we have all by now gotten, are very hard to get rid of. I decide to cut the children's hair. Vlaho's hair is easy to cut, I have done it before. When I get to Ivana, I have second thoughts. Should I cut it short or leave some length – after all she is a girl. In the end I decide to leave some length. In a couple of days my husband's cousin comes to visit; she is a professional hairdresser, so she takes care of the rest of us, making it easier to maintain at least a minimal level of hygiene.

A convoy called "Libertas" is coming to Dubrovnik, so we hear on the radio. They will attempt to break through the naval blockade, leaving on 28th October from Zagreb to Dubrovnik, by way of Split and Korčula. The convoy manages to sail into the port of Gruž on the 31st. 39 vessels follow the lead ship. The people are glad, some sense of relief arrived with the convoy, but it all blows out very soon. Many of the Croatian political leaders have arrived with the convoy. They held their speeches and left the very same day, leaving us on the mercy of the enemy. Nothing changes.

I am deeply concerned about my husband and also about his mother. It has been very long since he visited, or indeed since I had any news of them. I leave it all in the hands of God, loosing all hope.

1st November brings nothing but more attacks. They are very fierce now, and concentrated solely on city quarters. The attack continues the next day. Hotels on Babin Kuk are being severely bombed. I think to myself: "Thank God that we are here, instead of in one of the hotels. Who knows what would happen to us!"

The "Orlando" bakery is hit. It has been working all this time, making bread and supplying stores all over Dubrovnik. The stores open very early in the morning, especially for this time of the year. These are basically the safety measures for the bakers, store clerks and for the general population. We buy a three day supply of bread. Of course, we always eat the one that has already dried up, because the fresh one is kept in case there is none to buy. Some flour is kept in the house, for even rainier days than these, even though the gas is nearly spent. We have had an addition to our numbers at the end of October. Aunt's brother came with his family, so there are twelve of us in the house now, even though they have been placed in a different apartment. Days are getting much tougher, so we are all scuttled in our corners, hoping this would all just blow over. The attacks have increased in both frequency and intensity. Detonations are constantly heard all around. There is no mercy. Only vehicles with special permits are allowed to drive.

4.11. We are watching the fort of Imperial being hit directly. Parts of the City are also being hit. We do not move out of the shelter at all. We hardly manage to get some food and water from the small kitchen next to the room. The kitchen is covered by a single concrete slab so we cannot stay there when the situation gets tougher. The telephone is in there, making it quite dangerous to have a phone conversation during an attack. If the telephone happens to ring, the bravest person answers and then runs back to the shelter quickly.

The telephone rings in the evening and I am told that the call is for me. The voice is not familiar. A woman I know introduces herself and says: "Tonći is on Pelješac, he is well, don't ask me anything else." She hangs up. All tension, suffering and pain flow down my cheeks in full intensity. Nobody can stop my tears. "Why, oh God, why?!" What is happening. My husband said to me on leaving: "If anything happens to make me leave Orašac, I'll join you in the city."

I go out in front of the house so that nobody could see me cry. Aunt comes and tries to console me. I find it very hard. We are all alive, but so far from one another. I tell the children that daddy is well. I know where the woman who called lives and so I am determined to learn more. On my insisting she gives me her phone number. I dial the number countless times. The lines are so bad, but my persistence pays off.

I get through at about 9 PM. I ask to speak to my husband. On hearing his voice, I cannot speak for a while. All I can say is : "Tonći, tell me how and why Pelješac?" The same answer again: "It is not time for explanations. I'll call you." I accept my destiny and tell the children that daddy sends his love and that he is well. Since that day we heard from each other rather often during the next fifteen days or so. He has temporarily joined the ranks of the National Guard in Ston.

6.11. This has been the strongest attack on Dubrovnik so far. They are shooting from the sea and the land. Everything and anything seems to be the target. We do not leave our shelter for days, only for a moment to get water. I feel sorry for the children, but then I think that there are people worse off than us and that gives me some solace. We feel safe here. It is dark as we do not dare remove the stacked mattresses from the windows kept there during attacks. In case a shell lands under a window, they will slow the shrapnel penetrating into the room. Everybody has moved out from around our house. Panic has driven almost everybody into the shelter of the fort of Revelin, the central shelter for Ploče and the City. At one point, when fear becomes unbearable, our host says that we shall all have to go and sleep in the Revelin. I am in panic. There are already hundreds of people there, there is hardly an inch of free space there. How can I put my children to bed on a concrete floor? There are no old blankets to take. However, we give up that plan and bravely stay in on our own in that part of the town.

As always, nights are the hardest. I kiss my children good night and put them to bed which has to be made every night. They sometimes help. I listen with concern about the number of women and children leaving the city. Sometimes, I panic. Is it, perhaps, better for me to leave as well? Do I have the right to decide on behalf of innocent children to stay in this hell? Ships come and go.

I remain like a rock. I am staying in this town under Srđ; after all, I am not alone, there are other brave mothers with children.

My son is ill again, he has a fever. I have a cold myself, but have managed to stack up some medicaments and I am not afraid.

7.11. The Yugoslav army has issued an ultimatum for the Croatian army to lay down its arms and surrender by 6 PM. Expecting the worst, we are silent, everyone scuttled in own corner. Only my son is persistent in building a tower out of playing cards.

That whole night the City is lit by flare rockets all the time. We sleep very little, fearing what might happen. Thank God, dawn is here again. Bosanka, Srđ and Lokrum are attacked again in the afternoon. Shells whistle over our house from all directions. We have learnt to recognize the sound of a mortar, a gunboat and a tank.

9.11. early morning /6.50 AM/ the curfew is over. The peace is not long-lasting since the general alarm is sounded again at 7.25. Gruž and Lapad are under attack. A lot of boats and small vessels are on fire. We hear on the radio that hotels "Dubrovnik Palace", "Tirena", "Argentina", Belvedere" and "Libertas" are hit.

Shells are falling on Pile and the City itself. The fortress on mount Srđ has been hit by cluster bombs thrown from planes. Lokrum is also targeted. Hell itself is let loose. Just then, a telephone rings. Nobody wants to leave the safe corner. The bravest goes to the phone. It is for me again. Who is calling me in this hour of hell? An acquaintance from the general hospital is calling to say that if the little boy is ill he will send an ambulance. I don't understand it at all; who had told him that Vlaho is ill. Among other things he says: "Tonći is setting on his way to the city tonight." I cannot go on talking as it is too dangerous, the outside din being terrifying. I cut off the conversation and retreat in to my hiding-hole, even unhappier. How is daddy to break his way to us? In the presence of gunboats? All I know is that he had sailed from Orašac to the island of Šipan in a small boat. And, of course, overnight, past the gunboats.

I am stricken with panic. Now that it is a little more peaceful, I try to call Ston, but with no success. The lines are out of order. I want to tell him not to come into this hell. We are constantly warned over the radio not to move about as there are masses of unexploded mines. It is too dangerous to move anywhere. I am facing a night of pain and expectation. I must not show the children the extent of my fear for their father. I do not feel like talking to anybody.

We go to bed early as usual. I wait for everything to be quiet and then start to pray, reciting my rosary. I pray long into the night, praying to God to save our daddy. Tears flow down the face, slowly and quietly. Not a wink that night.

10.11. Dawn is here. As soon as the day breaks, detonations start on all sides. Lapad and Gruž are particularly fiercely attacked. Hotel "Belvedere" is hit from the gunboat and is in flames. Boats are ablaze again in the port of Gruž. Hotel "Argentina" has been hit again. Alarm sirens are all damaged. The hell still reigns. My husband is not arriving or calling from anywhere. Black thoughts are flashing through my head. Where is he heading? Where is he? Is he alive at all? At this moment, nobody can come near the City, it is too dangerous.

The day goes on. We find that the space of less than ten square feet is quite sufficient. The toilet is too far, but really only six - seven paces from us. That is a dangerous place too, with only one layer of concrete covering it. Vlaho needs to pee so often. I shout at him to hold back, he seems to be spending hundreds of years in the toilet. I bring my daughter a small ice-cream can to use in her corner.

Are we going to live through this hell? Is there an end to this? We all think and wish the same.

Uncle has gone to work and cannot come back. It is too dangerous. There are only women in the house now, apart from my son, but he is only a little boy. Uncle calls in the afternoon to say that he has been wounded while making sandwiches for refugees. Cooked meals cannot be served under such conditions. Luckily, he is only lightly wounded. I am worried about him, but I do not stop wondering where my husband is. Children are bored and keep asking me to spread something on their bread. I bring a slice of bread and margarine for each of them. Vlaho wants more. I whisper to him that he cannot have it. I am uneasy as we are not at home. He accepts his predicament and goes on being quiet in his corner.

The radio still remains our only link to the outside world. Night falls slowly. Attacks slacken, while my heart is ripped with pain. Where is my husband? Why did they tell me that he was coming? It almost seems better not to know anything. Another long and painful night. Prayers and tears. I plead to Our Lady for help and a happy outcome. I vow to do penance, to walk on my bare-feet to Her church when we return home if he comes back alive. It is day now and I lose all hope. I suppose that my husband had set out for the city from the island of Kalamota in his boat under the cover of the night. I am afraid that he is wounded and is floating in his boat somewhere on the open sea, wounded or dead. I have no hope left now.

New attacks from the break of dawn. The City is being hit. Hotels also. Around 8 o'clock, the telephone rings. They are saying: "Anita, Tonći is calling you!"

Is it possible? "Tonći, where are you?" – I shout into the receiver. "Don't worry, I am in Lapad. I'll come tonight." he says briefly. I cry with tears of happiness. Forgot to ask who he was staying with, but it is of no importance now. He is alive and that is all that matters. Detonations and the City in flames keep us from falling into each other's arms.

I embrace the children telling them that daddy is coming home tonight. Children are overjoyed as we have not seen him for over a month. The day is long and hard, but I feel great relief.

Hotels Excelsior, Argentina, Tirena and Imperial are hit. Boats in the port of Gruž are aflame, the island of Lokrum is hit. The Orlando bakery is also hit again. The City is without drinking water. Curfew starts at 9 PM.

Seven o'clock is drawing nearer but there is no sign of Tonći. "What has happened?" If only I knew where he was calling from. Minutes are years to me. It is 8 o'clock, but he is not here. Fright takes me over. The day has been hard. What if something has happened to him? Tension grows. Uncle is trapped at Babin Kuk, wounded, Tonći is not arriving! Children have gone to bed. I am waiting for him, Auntie keeping me company. Minutes are ages. I am nervous and silent as I watch the door that does not open. My head nods with exhaustion and heavy thoughts.

At 8.35 someone knocks on the door. The door opens slowly and my husband comes in. Unshaven, untidy, exhausted and sweating from walking. I jump towards him. I don't know when I was so happy and upset at the same time. I send him to go and say Hello to the children who are still awake. We have been waiting for him so eagerly.

Tired from his exhausting journey he sits down and starts his story. He wants to tell us everything but there is so much.

He has been cutting his way through for two days and two nights. It was only possible to travel by night, daylight being too dangerous. It was impossible to go past so many gunboats and other perils awaiting. He came from Ston to the island of Lopud by a skimmer. The voyage had been full of danger. The southerly wind brought high waves, making the skimmer jump up and down widely and cut the darkness at the speed of lightening. They were ordered to take off their boots and crouch down holding firmly to the sides of the boat. Then they were taken from the island of Lopud to the hotel Neptun in Lapad in another boat.

It was extremely dangerous, but they all arrived in the city safely. That was the only route that any help in manpower could reach Dubrovnik. The Croatian Army was far more courageous and smarter then the enemy. Although almost unarmed, it managed to realize so many nearly unthinkable plans. We have been forsaken by the world and by Europe, but God and justice were on our side. He left Orašac together with the inhabitants who had tried to withstand the enemy practically unarmed. They kept night watch with hunting rifles and a few proper army rifles for nights on end. On St. Luke's Day, 18th October, he was almost killed as he was on duty in Brsečine, west of Orašac. A far stronger enemy had discovered their position and showered them with a machine-gun burst. The whole unit just managed to get out safely retreating through the thicket and the rocky ground towards Orašac. At that point they were ordered by the headquarters in the City to leave the place immediately. On asking how and which way, they were told to do what they thought best. Some wanted to take the way by land, which was clearly a trap. My husband proposed the way by sea which was somewhat safer, regardless of the enemy warships.

Thus they set off from Orašac in small boats under the cover of the dark night which was their only ally. They sailed across to the island of Šipan, then by skimmers, used only for military purposes, to Ston. From then on we were together. We shared sorrow and pain, and fear, and suffering, as there was no happiness. The momentary happiness of our meeting left us very quickly.

He told how difficult it had been to get to Ploče from Lapad. He set off early in the morning (6.30) from hotel Neptun to us at Ploče. After some 15 minutes he was stopped by the thunder of the first shells. He found his way quickly into one of the high rise buildings which served as a shelter. He spent the whole day there as the City was constantly bombarded through the day. Only when everything was quiet, did he decide to set on his journey to his family by a dangerous route at about 7.30 PM. On his way, through complete dark, he kept falling into the holes made by shells.

Behind him were Gruž and the port in flames. He was coming near Pile. A horrifying scene of the hotel Imperial in flames was in front of him. Hole after hole in the road and along the pavement.

At last, he arrived to the entrance into the City. The City gates are closed. The first sentry asks his documents wanting to know where he is going and why at such an hour. He explains that he is coming from the battlefield of Ston and that he had not seen his family for over a month. Wishing him good luck in getting to us, they let him carry on. Stradun is deserted and full of holes. He comes to the gate at Ploče. Again, a sentry, documents, questions. They let him carry on. And so in the last minutes before the curfew he arrives safely to us. It was only then that he realised the extent of danger that he had been through.

13th November, the first day of our life together in somebody else's home, had dawned. Detonations resound throughout the City and its suburbs. However, I feel a certain peace in my soul, I feel much easier. The children are happy, although they still have to crouch in their corner. Detonations are more frequent and stronger, but we are braver now. What bitterness in all that! The war is raging at the same pace, if not stronger, but we feel easier in our soul. If we get killed, at least we will be in the embrace of death together. The burden from my shoulders is evenly shared between us.

That day was particularly hard because of bombarding. A little food and the last pieces of dry bread are carried to the room which served as our bedroom, but also as the shelter. We carry the table in there also during one of the lulls and have our lunch there, expecting to be 99 per cent safe there. That day we run out of drinking water. What an irony in all that!

A shell landed in the fire station, not far from our house. We can hear drinking water trickling away from a cistern that has been hit. If only people knew how sad I was for that ordinary drinking water. The whole City is thirsty and unwashed. We have to find some way to cope with troubles. During the quiet periods, some people hurry to the sea to have a wash. We get some water from the pool by the house. Although it is muddy and yellow, full of autumn leaves, we boil and drink it in spite of its taste of rotting.

We are happy in the knowledge that some people do not even have such water these days. Luckily, we all survived, nobody got ill. We have zwieback and black tea as we have run out of bread, and nothing can be prepared in the midst of thunder and flash of shells. Still we are somehow relaxed in the realization that not a single shell has hit our house although they are falling all around.

At dusk, as customary, attacks slacken. We can breathe more easily and the pang of fear is relaxed. As usual, we listen to the news every hour. We are shocked by the damage done, by the number of the killed and the wounded. The night, like all nights so far, is full of fear and insecurity. Dawn arrives slowly, but comforting like the craving for freedom.

14.11. dawned gloomy and rainy. We look forward to each rain with joy like little children as we have good reason. Every rain filled up reserves, admittedly not drinkable, water in our pool. Until I collected rainwater I would wash my hair, then wash some clothes that were needed, in that same water. It was real art washing and rinsing clothes in less than a gallon and a half of water.

But, one gets used to everything. My thoughts often wander off to our home and our water tank full of water which was of supreme importance now. The day is relatively quiet although the sound for general alarm was given. Radio Dubrovnik brings the news that 4000 women and children, the sick and the elderly have sailed from the port of Gruž aboard "Slavija". The numbers themselves appall us as the capacity of the ship was far below them. To make things worse, the southerly wind is throwing high waves against the wounded walls of our city. Thanks to relative peace, we go out on the balcony and wait longingly for the ship which had to sail behind the island of Lokrum on its way to Zelenika.

The ship is forced to take that course as the Yugoslav Army has no mercy. We wait and our waiting pays off. Our hair is tangled by the strong southerly wind; merciless waves spring up and threaten the unhappy "Slavija". It looks as if the sea itself has joined the enemy. The ship pitches, rolls and fights against the raging sea. A man standing near me is a seafarer. With tears in his eyes, he concludes that the ship can hardly endure this ordeal. The tempest is too strong and her cargo too precious. We dry our tears and pray to God to save the innocent lives and bring the ship safely to its destination.

When the ship disappears behind the rocks, we run to our shelter and wait impatiently for the news. The ship did arrive safely to Zelenika. Imagine, what luck since she was actually forced to sail to that port.

Next morning, the weather calms down and the ship sails safely back and on to its final destination. Those were the days when one man suffered for all and all people suffered for one.

The same day /15.11./ the alarm for the end of general danger is sounded. This one lasted for six full days. We all sigh with relief. After some five – six days we can finally have a breath of fresh air, still only at the western side of the house. The eyes of the vultures are looking out for us, ready to attack unexpectedly. Such moments enable us to fill up our reserves of water and bring them within easy reach. Nobody dares go to the city to see the damage done by shelling.

Uncle arrives home that same day. He walks with difficulty, but is well considering what might have befallen him. He tells us what has happened to him in detail. He describes the tearing and the noise, the smoke and the fire in the hotel full of innocent women, children and the elderly. Some fall victim; others are left without their rooms and their scarce necessary belongings.

My children are happy to be able to peep out and get some fresh air, even if it does all boil down to a few square feet behind the house. One is constantly expecting a sudden attack. Tension is eased only when the shell explosions die down but these periods are usually short as the danger is always imminent. The radio brings all the news but we still expect more than it can tell us. There is always hope that the next news will be more extensive.

The Italian ship "San Marco" enters the port of Gruž the following day, bringing humanitarian aid, which opens a humanitarian corridor. Our host has ordered butane gas and some vegetables from Split. When he arrived to the port to collect his goods, he realized that someone had stolen one of the gas containers. The parcel with vegetables was torn, half the contents missing, but even that was good. We have fresh vegetables - carrots, lettuce and Swiss chard - for the first time in so long.

It took three days to make statistics of the refugees. Long lines of refugees stand outside the improvised local administration office at Ploče to where we reside temporarily. On being questioned about their material possessions, many happen to forget a lot of them. That is hardly surprising when their mere existence, ordinary drinking water and a bit of food are the most important things in the world at this moment. There are some experts in assessing the value of these possessions. It all has a rather serious atmosphere, but at the same time it looks rather sad in that complete confusion. The car, the boat, the house or the wine casket are of no value to me. It has all lost its value and meaning. The most important things in the world are our family and our lives.

We are worried about Granny who has remained on the occupied territory in Orašac. She has stayed to guard what we have acquired through the years, from generation to generation and with a lot of work and hardship. There is no news from that part of the world. However, rumors are abundant, from the worst to the most optimistic. A new war of nerves is starting. Our little family is together, but our thoughts fly constantly to Granny, to our home. The warm sunshine increases the feeling of nostalgia in our souls. I wish so fervently that it would cast its warmth on me in front of our house, not here, in this strange place.

Day after day, foreign ships sail in. They bring humanitarian aid, medicaments and drinking water, and on leaving, take women, children and the elderly. In a moment, I catch myself thinking that our city is going to be deserted. Is a single mother or a single child going to stay in the city that has become the largest concentration camp in the world? Every time a ship leaves and I hear about the number of refugees it is carrying away, I feel pangs in my heart. I am never too sure whether I am right in being so determined in my wish to stay in the city.

Anyhow, whom will our brave guys defend if we all move out! We are giving them moral support through our staying. The radio tells us that the inner city is surrounded by land mines and so any movement in that area is strictly forbidden. For days, an appeal to help and save the city is being sent out into the world.

We carry on living our sad refugee life without our own identity. We are often upset by various discussions, political or moral. Many a time, I do not agree with the ideas of our hosts, but I rather remain quiet than cause a dispute. I thought it better that way for all of us since the situation is becoming tenser every day. I remember an old proverb saying: "One who remains quiet - teaches two." That seems like the only solution at the time. In any case, all discussions have no value at all in comparison with our longing for home and freedom. My children have become so disciplined. They are used to a little of quiet play and endless hours of silence, to early bedtime and early rising. In less than two months they have suddenly grown up, matured and adapted to everything they were not used to. They are happy to eat secretly a couple of raisins received from the humanitarian aid, or a few biscuits of the same origin.

Since we have had a couple of days of calm, I set of to the shop to buy some instant cocoa drink powder for the children. When I get to the shop at Ploče full of trepidation, walking through rubble and broken glass, I discover that it is closed due to damage. I have to go to other shops in town, some three hundred yards from Ploče. I seem to be walking for three miles, but I have to buy something to put in my children's milk. In any case, the milk we manage to get is of powdered kind and very poor quality.

The City is badly damaged and I have to hop over piles of broken glass and stone. I am surprised to find that almost all the shops are closed. With all that bombing, it is a wonder that they are still there. Only a few are conducting business in difficult conditions.

I look for what I need from shop to shop and find it eventually. I feel relieved. On my way back a reporter of New York Times accompanied by one of our reporters stops me in the street under the vault. When he asks me if I speak English, I think he needs help in getting around the City. I have no choice, but answer to a couple of his questions. When he asks if I am afraid for my children and why I have not left Dubrovnik, I say: "Of course, I am afraid, but this is my city where I and my children were born. I work and live here and no other city can replace my homeland." He put a few more questions to me, but in panic and hurry I start mixing English and German so the local reporter has to step in to my rescue.

In any case, I am struck by the eerie state of the City. I hurry to get to our temporary home as quickly as possible since that is the only place where I feel safe. I do not go to work as only a small number of people are working in this situation. All services, not necessary for keeping the life in the city on the go, have ceased to work. Our wages have been very low, and, in any case, my husband has been laid off on 15ᵗʰ April 1991, and was waiting to restart.

One of the more important news is that a boat service has been established between the port of Gruž and Mokošica. This is, so far, one of major signs of progress. First passengers start for Mokošica on 23ʳᵈ November. My husband is wandering around the city in the hope to learn something about Orašac and the people held there. He comes back feeling sad at not getting any news anywhere.

It is possible to spot truck and car headlights from Babin Kuk at night. It is the Yugoslav Army going about the place.

We are very disappointed with Radio Dubrovnik giving such detailed news about Župa Dubrovačka and, yet, very little about the western suburbs. Later on, we learn that it is not their intentional fault, but the fact that they are not getting any news from there. These days, strong winter has arrived. A thick layer of ice covers the water in our pool. We do not have any means of heating, but, fortunately, the room where we are spending our days is mostly underground and so keeps its own natural temperature. We are cold, but not too cold. At half past four in the afternoon we light the oil lamp, using our last supply of lamp-oil as it cannot be bought anywhere. In this war-time certain goods acquire importance which they never had in the time of peace. These are matches, lamp-oil, candles, batteries, and so on.

Italian, Greek and French ships are bringing aid to the port of Gruž. The Italian tanker "Simeto" has brought 11 tons of drinking water. It is a precious cargo for the city at this time. Our host, touched by the news, cries in his corner. Visibly shaken, he says: " Imagine, the Italians bringing water to us! Oh, God, is it possible that we have come to this?" People of the city have got used to anxiety, fear and the minimum of living standard. Above all, the most important thing is to stay alive. Our monotonous, sad and anxious living goes on from day to day. The children are accustomed to the minimum of space, no toys and silence for a considerable part of the day. I have bought a small plastic boat for Vlaho but he cannot play with it in the pool as the plastic material would, allegedly, spoil the water. He looks at it so sadly as he pulls it along the concrete instead on the water.

Soon after 1st December, children are invited via the local radio to come to the Rector's Palace on St. Nicolas's to decorate the Christmas tree and receive presents. It never crosses my mind to take my children there since danger is lurking any minute. Anyhow, it is more important to stay alive and well. A small chocolate and an orange at this moment are a sign or great care, but also a very void gesture.

At this time I am going around the shops since I am entitled to a consumer credit at a low interest rate. No children clothes could be found so I bought some for us adults. Anyway, I have lost so much weight that the few clothes I still possessed do not fit me any longer.

That day, blankets were distributed to refugees but we did not manage to get them as they had all gone. Our hosts are very angry as, naturally, we have been using their blankets. I feel humiliated and my son is very sad, too. I tell him solemnly: "I'll buy you some blankets, son, you will not sleep without covers."

Even though it is all said in the heat of the moment, it hurts terribly. We get our blankets the day after. I must admit that I feel very humiliated then. These blankets must be from some military reserves. They do not even look like household blankets. We have been humiliated and mistreated for a long time now, and I am again shocked by unimportant matters.

I take those brown blankets that are not even properly hemmed. They seem more suitable for horses than for people. Europe spent holidays in the sunny Dubrovnik, but even so they must have taken us for horses.

It is quite cold these days, since we have no other choice, these blankets will do. Anyhow, I have my own blankets now; they are mine even if they are ugly.

5.12. I went to town before St. Nicolas's Day to buy some stuff and use up the rest of my credit. When I start on my way home, I spot groups of people in between the City walls, not moving any further. Luckily, I come across the former head accountant from my firm who told me that two women have been wounded at Ploče gate. I get scared as that is my only way home. Snipers are controlling the eastern exit from the city so that anyone passing through puts his life in danger. I carry on. The port of Revelin is used as a shelter and is a little further on. I stop there, waiting for an hour and a half. People are anxiously grouping around the door. Hardly anybody dares cross the wooden part of the bridge, only some fifteen feet long, and its maybe twice as long stone section. Everybody wants to cross to the other side, but it is too dangerous. However, every five minutes, someone takes the daring step. I have been watching all that and after two hours decide to run across. If I am hit, I cannot help it, I have to get home to my children. My heart beats in fear, my feet stumble. Holding my plastic bag firmly in my hand, I start running in the zigzag fashion across the bridge. Danger is lurking all the way home from the other side of the bridge which shuts of the view from Bosanka. Luckily for me, nothing happens, except for the adrenalin rush in my blood. This is an unbelievable feeling of relief. I cross the first, most dangerous section. There are now some three hundred feet of less dangerous ground to cover. I run it all from a house to a wall and vice versa. On arrival home, I hear from my husband that he has heard it all on the radio and was very concerned for me.

St. Nicholas Day, 6th December. Traditionally, on this day children would get small gifts and start decorating the Christmas tree. Not so this year. From the crack of dawn all the parts of the city are being bombarded heavily. This date marks the most severe attack on Dubrovnik's Old City. Grenades are coming from everywhere – from gunboats, artillery weapons, tanks... we cannot figure out where the grenades flying over our heads are coming from.

Twelve have lost their lives on the same day; over sixty wounded. The stone cross on Srđ has been torn down, after withstanding the attacks for so long. Truly a day out of hell. I have covered my children's heads with pillows to ease the fear that the sounds of detonations bring with them. Sections within the walls were burning. When all was quite in the evening, we crawl out of our shelter and look at the Town, the pearl of the Adriatic as it was once called, being consumed by flame. Boats and barges are burning in the old port. The clamor of fire fighters can be heard.

My husband got a fever. He has to take his medicine with cold water instead of warm tea. Our life has become too difficult. We decide it has been long enough – we have to find a room in a hotel that is not too devastated and move. We have been waiting for freedom and for international recognition for three months now. All we got were grenades, sadness and pain.

The next day Tonći goes looking for a room. It is impossible to find any accommodation in these sort of conditions. I do not want to go to Babin Kuk; whenever attacks start, hotels are hit. He walked for mils asking around. His brief answer was: "All filled to the capacity." He is exhausted and broken spirited. We run out of cooking gas. Luckily, there is some burning wood in the back of the house. Our kitchen is now an open fire in the back yard. An old pot is used for washing clothes. The greatest godsend is the water from the pool. It made us so happy! However, all these things are not enough to make us comfortable; we feel that we have worn our welcome out, even though no one has told us anything. We are sad and hurt. On top of everything else, we still know nothing of Tonći's mother. Life is reduced to an automatic performance of most essential chores. Few words are ever uttered, and silence is as devastating for us as the grenades are to our beloved city.

13th December dawns, gloomy and sorrowful, similar to so many in the near past. Still, there are differences. Our hostess heads to Orašac to see her mother. This was only the second ship the Yugoslav Army has allowed to leave the port of Gruž in the direction of Zaton. We have given her a letter and some money for my mother in law.

Impatiently, we expect her back. Uncertainties are grave and many with such a trip. Around 11 o'clock our hostesses' brother places a large bag in front of us, asking us whether we recognize it. We all look at him, blank expressions evident on our faces. Suddenly, Tonći's mother appears from behind a corner. Tears of joy start down our faces, I shake, as if in shock, not remembering shaking like this even during the attacks. She kisses and hugs us, the children with special care and tenderness, not even attempting to hide her tears. She has heard nothing of her son for over a month and a half. It has been hard living like that, not knowing whether he is alive or dead, where is he. She had also been fearing for me and her grandchildren, since she knew nothing of us either. We sit at the dinner table.

There is no time for a long talk we all so desire. The ship leaves at one-thirty and she has to be on it. She has expressed her hope, and we all agreed that perhaps we would be home for Christmas.

She told us of her long nights, filled with fear, alone in her house. At any moment she expected someone to break in and start shooting. She had a couple of bitter experiences, but she withstood everything heroically. She promises to come visit in a few days if nothing happens. We give her some raisins and a couple of fish cans.

She leaves sad, but her permit is only valid for a day. We are at ease now; we know that she is alive, though considerably exhausted and thinner. From that day on, my husband runs to the port every day, along with other people from the village, and waits for news. As long as we are all safe and accounted for we can stand all the toil and fear.

We are still searching for a room. We have to pull some strings, but we are informed that we will be given a room in hotel Vis 1, as soon as this one family moves out. My aunt and my cousins are also there with there families, so we are glad. My mother in law has visited us once more during our stay in uncle's house. When we told our hosts we were leaving to a hotel, that we felt we were too much of a burden to them they asked us what the rush was. We could, however, see the relief on their faces. This was no surprise, we were all on our last nerves. I am very glad to leave and look forward to freedom in a little hotel room. Children are a bit skeptical; they have by now gotten used to this place and to the people living in it. It was pretty hard for them to leave home once again, even if it was not our own. These pre-Christmas days are spent in the gathering of our meager belongings and dreaming of departure. All the trouble is easier to handle hoping for a soon departure. After some effort, we manage to get the key to our new home on 22nd December. A plastic red tag with a number on it, 353, and on it a key to our future room.

I kiss my children and tell them: "We are moving tomorrow." Ivana is not happy as she does not know what a hotel is, but Vlaho is looking forward to a change. The whole of the next morning is taken up with getting together of our poor belongings: a few clothes, footwear, refugee blankets, clothes-pegs and a plastic bucket. I am taking a cheese spread and three or four tins of fish from the humanitarian aid. I bought a packet of margarine and a jar of jam for the children. This represents a real treasure as first aid. Our plastic bags stand in a row, together with eight refugee blankets tied together with a rope. My husband's brother in law and his brother have come for us. We pack it all into a car and set off at 1:30, into the uncertain future once again. An old lady, who is staying there, sees us off with tears in her eyes. The landlady's brother with his family is also staying under their protection.

We arrive in Lapad in front of hotel Vis. It seems so gloomy and sad, but it is going to be our home from now on. In spite of difficult moments, I have gotten quite used to life in my husband's uncle's house. Our room is at the top floor of the hotel meaning that in these war conditions we have only one concrete slab above our heads. I shudder at the thought, but we had difficulty finding this.

It is a cloudy and dark day so, as there is no electricity, we need to make the beds as soon as possible. They have no bedding and no pillows for the children. What we found were

bare beds and two pillows, and there are four of us. My husband has an aunt in the city and he asks her for some bedding. The children have no pillows the first night, I put sweaters under their heads. The room is very cold. These less than two hundred square feet, including the bathroom are going to be our living quarters. I make a double bed for myself, for my husband and for our daughter, while our son gets an ordinary cot. There is nothing to put on that bed, so I fold two or three refugee blankets instead of a mattress. We do not get any hotel blankets as they have been distributed to other people before our arrival, so we have only our refugee blankets to cover ourselves with.

There is no glass on the balcony door. They are covered only with thin nylon. Although we cover ourselves with six or seven refugee horse blankets which are quite heavy, we cannot get warm. We shiver with cold like we never before in our life. My toes hurt from the weight of the blankets. We need to light a candle as early as 4 PM, and candles are so precious. There is no water but, fortunately, the sea is right below the hotel. We fetch sea water in buckets for the toilet, but it has to be carried up to the third floor. As it is unbearably cold, we go down to our cousins who are a floor below. They have been here for a month. It is much warmer in their room. The room is below two concrete slabs, and the mere presence of people makes it warmer. The first couple of days we would just sleep in our room as the cold is too great. There is some ice outside. In these moments our thoughts fly over to Orašac and our old fire stove.

People living in the hotel make a fire behind the hotel, under a wall. That is the way to warm the water for washing themselves and their clothes. Water is boiled in great big cans, obtained from the hotel (these are the cans that used for peas or French beans). Whoever wants to heat the water has to contribute to the supply of firewood. The children fit into this large community immediately. Corridors are unbearably cold. It is an old hotel, used mostly as summer holiday accommodation for workers. Our son comes to the aid of his parents the following day. He runs to the kitchen and brings two of the cans needed to fetch water or sea water. One of them is to be used as the washing machine. We make handles out of some wire and over the next three days acquire four or five cans which are kept on the balcony. All balconies are filled with cans, brooms and firewood used to make fires behind the hotel. The hotel looks like anything but a hotel.

The nylon on the balcony door shakes and lets the wind and the cold air into the room so that at times the curtain moves eight inches backwards and forwards. When asking at the reception desk for some nylon sheet we are told that there is not any. Vlaho is diligently bringing the sea water, his sister is too small for that. He has heard about the Red Cross and has put his sister on their list. He is very happy to bring her a chocolate and two jars of fruit pap. He is glad to be helpful.

24.12. Boxing Day dawns. It is the saddest Boxing Day in our lives. We should get our meals that day since we arrived in the afternoon the previous day and, not being entitled to a meal have some cheese spread for supper and go to bed. Word goes that stock fish is supposed to be served for lunch. The children never liked it. We sit down in the cold restaurant with windows shattered by detonations. We do not know anybody except for our cousins. A ball the size of a fist made of potato and bits of stock fish are placed on each plate. That food seems to be eating me, instead of me eating it. The children look sadly at that meal, but it is all that the house has to offer. I feel miserable. All we eat are three small doughnuts each. We leave the restaurant hungry and look for some bread and jam in our room for consolation.

We bought some salami and cheese for Christmas the following day. It was very expensive, but it makes us happy. We left the food on the balcony as it serves as the fridge. The side where our room is never gets any sun.

Father Christmas visits the hotel in the afternoon. The children are thrilled with Christmas carols in the cold reception area. The adults are mostly in tears. Home, sweet home – I think with longing. I hate the sight of the decorated Christmas tree at the reception hall; I hate the cold corridors and our cold room. Food is really poor. We supplement it in our rooms. There is Russian tea for breakfast, bread and jam. Sometime there is cocoa made with water, rather than milk. There is a piece of chicken back with potatoes and tea with a bit of bread for supper. The menu is the same for days. Chicken with rice, meaning chicken backs as these chickens for refugees do not seem to have breasts or legs.

I feel sorry for the children as our food is really poor, and there is nowhere to prepare anything as access to the kitchen is strictly forbidden.

And so Christmas Eve arrives. We go down to our cousins to share the joy and sadness of that holy night. They had gone fishing and caught a couple of squid that they had cooked on a gas ring in their room. They also have some bean salad and boiled potatoes and invite us to dinner. We look forward to that dinner since all we have in our room is some tinned fish and a bit of jam.

Our children join the others in singing Christmas carols round the hotel. They take a torch and run down dark corridors going from door to door and singing to people they do not know. They are truly grateful for every piece of candy and every orange they are given. I am afraid that my children might get lost, but the cousins calm me down saying that their children have been playing down hotel corridors for days. It is all strange to me and feels very cold. Cheerful children's voices approach the door. "In all seasons of the year.." children sing expecting an orange, a sweet or some money. Vlaho's voice that I know so well, stands out among the other ten. They come back after an hour of singing, happy and exhausted. They are carrying with them a plastic bag full of oranges, almonds and sweets. They are so sweet and fair as they share their goodies. Vlaho finds great pleasure in it.

After that first sad Christmas Eve we retreat to the solitude of our cold room No. 353. The number signifies our new home.

Christmas is here. By far the saddest one in our lives. People bow their heads going to breakfast. Grief has overcome all, and severe pain seems to be stabbing the refugee hearts. It was too dangerous to have midnight Masses anywhere in the city last night, so the whole celebration is basically reduced only to Christmas day. Hotels have organized Masses for the refugees. Ours is at 10:30. We are all distraught, but we put on our best clothes and go to the cold restaurant where Masses are usually held.

The priest attempts to offer some solace, but to no avail; there is no way to stop the tears of the congregation. There is no dry eye to be found in the room. My husband's uncle invites us for Christmas lunch. We are grateful, but not particularly glad. He comes to pick us up at one o'clock and we are once again at his place. Some tears are shed, but not for long. Something deep inside me kept telling me to endure. After lunch we return to a hotel full of coldness and grim faces of refugees. Under normal circumstances, on this day they would be seated at a splendid, rich table. Each person's mind flashes, if only for a moment, with images of last Christmas, so beautiful now. People simply barricade themselves in their rooms, waiting for this day to pass as soon as possible.

We do not have a radio, so we usually go to one of my cousins' room to learn some news of the situation on the front.

Still, this sad Christmas brings some glad tidings; on Christmas morning it has been announced that some parts of the city are going to get electricity, after being in the dark for 86 full days. The power line to Lapad has been damaged pretty badly, so we are not that lucky. We are all very jealous of hotel Kompas on the other side of the cove – they have a gasoline operated power plant of sorts. The hotel is lit every night. The next day it is time to do the laundry and to bathe. I take my can and pour clean water into it. Vlaho has patiently waited in line for it when the fire truck would come, generally once every two or three days. All chaos would break loose; my son was the only one among us who was patient enough to wait. So, I take the can of water and go behind the hotel where the fire is. An old iron grid serves as the cooker. Many cans are placed on it. I place my brand new can on the grid and after maybe ten minutes it is all black. After the water has boiled, the can has to be carried along the hotel corridors up to our fourth floor room. The water smells of smoke, specked with ash and charcoal. However, nothing can be done – this is the only way to heat the necessary water. We have to towel dry the hair as best we can; the sun does not shine on our terrace. The smell of shampoo and soap is overpowered by the smell of smoke. All the same, we feel clean.

Next time, the same can is used for laundry. I stuff the laundry in it and take it to the fire. We buy the detergent and basically everything else we need ourselves. The laundry suffers a similar fate – the ash falls into the can relentlessly. After the water has boiled, the laundry has to be rinsed in sea water first, and then in fresh water in the rooms. The balcony is miniscule, maybe twenty square feet. We have placed strings on the balcony, but our clothes would dry for several days, because walls surrounded this small enclosure on three sides, and we were facing north. The children had met new friends already. They would play together in the cold hotel corridors and in the back yard. I watch them closely, especially during these holidays. The enemy attack can happen any time, and I do not like them to go out.

A couple of days before the New Year, my mother in law arrives from Orašac. As I am standing at the reception desk, I notice my husband carrying a bag, his mother following closely. We are al so happy to see her. She has found out that we have moved to a hotel and she decided to visit us. We offer her with what little we have and on that very day, while she is with us, the lights come on. It gives us great pleasure, if it is only for a short a time.

We have not seen light for three months already. I pull a portable cooker from under the bed; I have borrowed it in case the power came. I plug it in and start making coffee, so happy for this little delight. The two or three hours pass so fast, and mother has to leave; she has to catch a boat and go home. The children are sad, but we have to say goodbye and see her off.

This New Year will be the first one in her life that she has welcomed alone, and under occupation. We have to accept it. Mother has brought some dried figs, some brandy and a couple of eggs. We have bought her some biscuits, some meat and two loaves of bread, so she would not tire herself, kneading her own bread and baking it in a fire furnace.

These days, leading up to the New Year, have also brought water to some parts of the town. This is also a reason for great joy. The water has started running in the ground floor of the hotel first. Naturally, the water has to climb two more floors before it arrives on ours. We are the last to get it and, of course, the first to loose it. As soon as the shout is heard: "The water is here!" everybody rushes to stockpile it into cans and canisters, some old and darkened by the flames, some new and shiny, and to arrange them on the balconies. It feels exhilarating to be able to flush the toilet or to wash up in the sink. As soon as the power was in, those in charge of hotel security have started making rounds and demanding total blackout. We would always put on just the lamp above the dressing cabinet. It was too much light anyway, our eyes having grown unaccustomed to light. Headache had been a regular occurrence during the first few days. We are all used to candle light by now, and our eyes are unhappy with anything else. The children are filled with joy when the power is back. We have acquired a portable radio, so we can hear the news. Radio Dubrovnik has started broadcasting all day long during the Christmas holidays. All seems well, except there is this longing for freedom and a heartfelt longing for our home.

Hotel has rules; according to them we are supposed to clean our rooms, hallways, restaurant, do the dishes etc. by ourselves. The reception desk and the kitchen are the only segments within the hotel functioning relatively normally; everything else is left to us. It has only been a few days since we have arrived, and I already see my name on the chore-board. I am supposed to do the dishes.

I ma secretly happy I was not assigned to do the dishes on New Year's Day, three days ago. Each team has to do all the day's dishes for two days. The second team cleans the reception area and the third one the restaurant. The first time it is my turn to do the dishes, there is no water or power yet. The dishes are washed in sea water, and rinsed with it as well.

As I enter the kitchen for the first time that morning I am affronted with the unpleasant smell of filth. The kitchen is mostly dug into the ground and very little can be seen. A single candle is burning behind our backs. My team consists of three other women, first timers like myself. We do not know where to star from. Three gallons of warm sea water and a little dishwashing detergent is all we have at our disposal to take care of all the breakfast dishes, on top of some left over from the dinner. I would be much happier had I not seen that. An urge to vomit rises from the pit of my stomach. This is indeed minimal hygiene. These three gallons of water have to suffice for about two hundred cups, seven or eight large, industry size cooking pots and about fifty plates. After the "washing", everything is rinsed in perhaps six more gallons of cold sea water and the dishes are considered clean.

After lunch, the things are even worse. The same amount of water is supposed to take care of the dishes used by 250 persons at lunch. The unpleasant smell emanating from the kitchen makes me queasy, considering the fact that we eat out of these dishes does not help at all. From that day on, we do not go to the restaurant to eat. I have managed to get some dishes to our room, so we eat there. My son and I usually bring the meals up to the room – breakfast, lunch and dinner together. There is no table in our room, so we eat off the bedside cabinets and our knees. There are two chairs to the four of us. Us grownups, we sit, slanting our backs, because the bedside cabinet is so low, and the children eat standing up. I wash my dishes in the bathroom. I have a cooker, and I heat some water on it, together with some liquid detergent. The kitchen staff is most unkind, the cleaning crew rude and ill-mannered. They are paid their salary, and do nothing. They are only in the hotel for an hour or two; they take a stroll through the hotel, having coffee with the people they have met, and then they leave. Waiters are also very moody, if the mood is good, then everything is OK. If it is not, beware. Mostly, they are in a lot of hurry to get home. I notice some of them hiding the lute they have taken from the kitchen in their pockets or behind their backs. The only commendable people working in the hotel are the reception desk staff. They are very patient and kind. All the rest of them are better to be avoided. They consider us intruders and only take care of their own personal gain. I clearly remember seeing one of the restaurant staff insulting the older women in the milk line he was overseeing one afternoon. "Isn't it beneath you to drink this industry product," he kept asking them, "What with all the milk your cows give?" The women bowed their heads and kept waiting.

The lounge area is alive since the electricity has arrived. The television is working; some people are playing chess, the other cards. Younger men are mostly busy at the front, returning to their families in the hotel after their missions are accomplished. The others have duties and responsibilities taking care of the needs of refugees. The children run happily about and play. Our joint misery has taught us to be and act as one big family. Life goes on, no matter what.

Right about these days, the Red Cross starts handing out clothes. We have not been informed of anything upon our arrival at the hotel. My cousin's wife takes me to select some clothes. I decline, even though my daughter only has one pair of pants. Her second pair was ripped during the winter. Vlaho's clothes are no better. She insists, so I follow. As we arrive in the winter swimming pool are, I see clothes scattered all around. I feel so pitiful and humiliated. Am I supposed to find something for my children to wear in the midst of all these hand-me-down rags? I dive in, utterly appalled, looking specifically for two pairs of slacks. She keeps handing me these sweaters and shirts. I put them back on the pile, insisting only upon slacks. The feeling of basic humiliation fills me. People who have been living in the hotels for a while are used to this. Some of them have lost their homes and everything within them, so this was the way for them to get dressed.

Some time between Christmas and New Year the Red Cross has started handing out gifts for the children – used toys, shipped through the humanitarian aid channels, and some candy. Ivana is so happy clutching a stuffed bird and candy. Her brother follows, rather darkly. He was among the last ones to receive his gift. "If you wait patiently, you will get the better gift.", someone in the line has told him. He did as he was told and, of course, his gift was one of the worst. All he got were some plastic action figures and some wooden rings, which would be far more appropriate for a baby. His anger and disappointment make me sad, but I know that the honest ones usually get this sort of treatment in life.

Sometime around New Year the banks started exchanging the Yugoslav currency into Croatian. More lines – this time in front of the banks. New Year's Eve has arrived. More sadness and suffering, painful memories of home, Christmas trees and the voices of children caroling. The only pleasure consists of water and electricity. As soon as we had gotten electricity, the hotel staff organizes a raid of sorts. Nobody is allowed to have a cooker, space heater, iron or any kind of electrical appliance. This is an act of utter selfishness on the part of these people who cannot find it in themselves to have pity on the elderly or indeed on the children. There are even babies in the hotel. For days on end they stare into the worn faces of people who are without home, while they themselves, in their warm homes, enjoy the benefits of civilized life. They forbid us to plug the cooker in to heat some milk for our children.

Of course, for a parent, the well being of a child is much more important than the cruelty of hotel personnel. After warming the milk (which I have bought myself) for the children, or baking some eggs, I would hide the cooker under a stone slab on the balcony.

The answer to the hotel housekeeper's question about owning a cooker was always negative. We have learned to hate their hideous and selfish expressions. Their Christmas trees are decorated and home made cookies await them. Our children have to get by on a box of biscuits their parents have bought.

This raiding the rooms lasted for quite awhile. I am always fearful that someone will knock on the door while the cooker is plugged in. Luckily, the refugee leader has protested this practice, so they back off a bit. Are we not allowed to at least try and make our life bearable? This is, after all, our home for the time being. Everybody is obliged to take the best possible care of the assigned living space and has to take responsibility for all the possible damages. It is easier after that; I do not have to dread each footstep or a sound of talking coming from the corridor. There are two vacuum cleaners available for the whole hotel. I consider myself lucky if I get to use it once every seven or eight days for about half an hour. I usually sweep the wall-to-wall carpeting with a broom, washing it with a damp cloth afterwards.

Just before New Year I find a message at the front desk: my boss is telling me to report to work on 2nd January. The electricity has finally made it possible for us to start working. I am not happy about leaving my children in the hotel; we have just started getting used to the new living arrangement. New Year goes by, basically just a rerun of Christmas, marked by the gloomy faces of refugees. Vlaho and Ivana run around the corridors, playing with their new friends. Not far from our hotel, in the hotel Splendid, an unofficial school has started. Vlaho wants to go, but we do not allow it. The danger of attacks is still very realistic. We like to be together.

According to the house rules, the children are allowed to play until 7:30 PM; that is when the central news is broadcast on TV. I respect this rule, so my children have to be in the room by 7. Many a time my son was begging me to stay a little longer. I call this rule "The Kid's Curfew" and am enforcing it, not wanting to be one of those sloppy parents who are always breaking the rules.

Right after New Year I go to work. Breakfast starts at 7:30 and lasts till 8:30. Since my bus leaves at 7:35 I am not able to get breakfast. I work from 8 to 2 every day including Saturdays, because of all the missed months of work. I miss the children very much, I hate leaving them in that place. I return to the hotel at about 2:30. After getting of the bus in front of the hotel the hardest thing for me is passing the chill reception area and the already half dirty hallways to my room. After I enter the room and see the faces of my loved ones, it is much easier. Lunch is distributed from noon to 1. After that it is impossible to get anything. Vlaho would usually get the lunch around 12, and that lunch, low quality at its best, would wait for me completely cold. It was good if the lunch consisted of something that can be heated. Mostly, however, this is not the case. I eat very little of the petrified meal and then I get to cleaning the room. The exact same is repeated every day. My children bring me the only glimmer of joy in this maddening routine. Their cheerful faces give me courage and strength, forcing me to hang in.

January is very cold. It took quite awhile to get the central heating system working. The heating would start at 5 PM, and end promptly at 7. Surprisingly, these two hours are enough to warm the rooms at least a bit. The radiator is also very useful for drying the clothes. With the central heating came another "luxury" - twice a week there is warm water for about two hours. This temporarily cheers everyone up a little bit.

Every night we gather in front of the TV, following the news in dead silence. There has been talk for days of the possible recognition of Croatia by the international community. News consists, as expected, only of war and pain and suffering. Then, at last, on 15th January 1992 the day comes. Our tired ears do not believe it – our country is officially recognized as an independent political entity. People break into a spontaneous applause, shaking hands and hugging each other. Happiness fills a previously cold space. Everyone thinks: "This is the end to our pain and suffering!" At that moment it seems like we are all going to go to our homes tomorrow. We are bitterly wrong. All the world has done for us consists of caring for the protection of cultural monuments and sending humanitarian aid. The enemy has taken no heed to an occasional cry to stop the destruction of Dubrovnik. The glum monotony of refugee life is to be our fate for a while longer.

Mother visits us from Orašac every two weeks, bringing us some much needed things and clothes. Vlaho is very diligent. Each morning he brings breakfast, and also lunch and dinner at noon.

He wants to be useful. I go to work every day.

The feast of St. Blaise (Vlaho) is approaching. It is the central feast of the Church calendar in our diocese. It is Vlaho's birthday on the day before. We gather up courage and take the children to church on the day of the feast. We even watch the traditional church banners being flown in greeting to the saint. It is all filled with sadness and melancholy. I am scared the whole time, fearing the attack which could have happened at any time. We take the children to have some cake in the pastry shop. We buy the last ones we find. The prices are very high and the offer very poor. This is true of basically anything being sold in the city these days. We return to the hotel, glad that nothing bad has happened.

By that day we have heard the news that it has been decided that school would start in all the city schools. Our son starts third grade. His books are left in Orašac, so we write a letter to Granny, asking her to send them. He will have to do without them for a few days. When the books arrive, he is happy to start school properly, the way other children have. He likes the children very much, but he is particularly fond of his new teacher. Her name is Mrs. Marija Čeović, and she is a refugee as well, coming from Konavle, a region to the east of the city. The class starts off with only sixteen students, but before February is over they are up to thirty-two. It must have been very difficult working with so many strange children, but Vlaho is at the very top right away. I am very proud of him as he comes home happy, saying that the teacher said he did best at something. He has always been a very sociable, communicative and bright child. He was excellent in the previous two grades.

The school program has to be done in a very brief period of time. None of this high-speed studying seems hard to him. He pays attention in class and picks things up very quickly. There is no desk or table in our room for him to study at. He does his homework sitting on the floor, his notebook on the bedside cabinet. He studies very briefly, maybe for twenty minutes, and then skips along with his friends to the hotel yard. I am amazed, thinking to myself: "I don't think I could do this well at this fast a rate!" For the first month or so he does not have a school bag, so he carries his books in a nylon bag. The handles often break, not being able to support the weight. There is no school bag to be bought in all of Dubrovnik, so we, once again, write a letter to Granny to send us his old school bag from Orašac by boat.

Pretty soon, the flu comes to visit the hotel, not skipping a single room. Coughs and sighs are heard through the thin walls. Vlaho catches it first, followed by me and Ivana. All three of us are in the bed at the same time, our temperature seldom under 104. I am angry at myself for falling ill at the same time as the children, for not being able to help them. My head is spinning and my head hurts severely. I am completely helpless. My son asks for help to go to the bathroom and I try to get up but I immediately feel nauseous. I am not even able to help my children that much. Fortunately, my husband manages to stay healthy and plays the nurse to all of us. The hotel food can barely sustain the healthy. The cooker is a blessing and my husband makes us some chicken soup. We eat several spoons of soup and that is it for the day. The smell of meat makes us all sick, and we have to even force the soup down.

The biggest problem is that the room cannot be properly aired. It is very cold outside and we are sick and sweaty with fever. The flu is very powerful and all of my bones and joints ache. The beds are no help either – we are lying on some old bumpy mattresses which make the bones sore even without the flu. Vlaho's bed is the worst. He sleeps on a cot that is covered only with the dreaded refugee blankets and he often complains of back pains. The fever lasts for some five or six days and we slowly begin to recover. The Red Cross is handing out oranges these days, but someone has to go to the ground floor to get them. The flu has worn me out so badly that I cannot go to the ground floor for a week after recovering. I am sorry about the oranges; they are exactly what we need. Luckily, my husband is healthy so he takes care of us. He buys fresh fruit for us and makes us soup every day.

Vlaho looses ten days of school, but he catches up very quickly. I sometimes find all the praise coming from his teacher a little hard to believe, since I know how little time and effort he put into his studies. I go to school to talk to his teacher and find that every single word is true. His teacher tells me that she is very happy with him, that he is very polite and bright and extremely attentive in class. His tests are usually excellent. We are both very happy and proud of him. The hotel has organized a kindergarten by mid February. The teachers from nearby kindergartens have offered to volunteer their time. The children are very happy, and so are the parents, especially the ones who have to go to work. The children have an opportunity to spend their time usefully and they are safe. The kindergarten is situated in one of the former recreation halls next to the kitchen, so it is fully under ground. I have to go to work each day and my husband goes to the harbor to get groceries, and also to get some news from the docking boats. The children would sometimes be alone for two or three hours. Each time when we have to leave them alone we lock the balcony door to prevent them from falling. Vlaho has a duty to watch over his little sister until Daddy comes back. He knows where to hide in case of danger. I had arranged for my aunt and cousin to take care of them in case of the emergency. Vlaho always pays attention to what he is told and waits in the room patiently for our return. He plays with his sister, even though he is drawn to the clutter of his friends in the hotel yard. When the kindergarten finally opens, he is happy to take his sister down, and take her back at 2. He finds great pleasure in these little responsibilities, in the fact that he is her big brother. He goes to school in the meantime, at hotel Adriatic, just across the road.

All the entertainment happens in the evening hours. The nights are still rather long, and we pass the time by playing chess, dominos, or some other board game. The news broadcast is listened to on the radio, and the central TV news is never skipped. Those few hours in the evening we forget the drudgery of our collective lives. As I have been spending most of my days at work for a while now, I get very upset when I see my name on the dishwashing or cleaning list. Some of the others are starting to rebel, too. We work honestly for our minimum wage and the cleaning crew and some of the kitchen staff successfully manages to delegate their work load to the refugees. One time Vlaho was running a fever again and I was supposed to go to the kitchen to do the dishes. I obey the order for two straight days and then I decline. Half of their food defies eating, anyway, and I have my own dishes which I wash in my room. After all, the work ought to be done by those who get paid for it or, in the worst case, the refugees who are unemployed.

This problem is finally solved, and to our satisfaction. The dishes are supposed to be done by the hotel employees, and the cleaning crew has to keep the hotel clean. Cleaning the rooms and hotel corridors remains our duty. The electricity would go out, sometimes for a couple of days at a time, water as well, so our life is made a little more difficult again. The sea water and fire trucks are a part of our life again.

Another visitor comes in March. This time it is the chickenpox. They arrived with the children who were slowly coming back to Dubrovnik with their mothers from Rijeka, Opatija and other places. They would talk of excellent food, fruit and all sorts of desserts being served with their meals. I get very worked up over this. Our food is inadequate, even though the government is paying a lot of money for the refugees to be fed. In other cities refugees are living basically as tourists and, for the same money, we are practically starving.

There is no chance of my children escaping chicken-pox. Rash soon develops, as well as the fever. They have to stay in the room for a fortnight, having no contact with anyone. I am so furious. Why do they have to get every possible disease which comes within a fifty-mile radius? They just lie in bed for the firs few days. Once again, the problem is fresh air. Chicken-pox patients cannot be cooled. Later, they play in the room. I sympathize with them, realizing that being quarantined in the room for fifteen days cannot be easy for them. Vlaho misses a lot of school, once again.

There is a boy from his class in the hotel and he regularly comes to fill him in on he progress in the studies. The boy has already had chicken-pox, so there is no fear of him becoming ill. Vlaho diligently copies everything from his notebooks and keeps up with the schoolwork. The chicken-pox have, combined with the flu, seriously damage my children's immune system.

The daylight is getting longer and the longing for home gets stronger. Mother still comes regularly and brings us fresh vegetables, eggs and cheese. She stays for two or three hours and tells us of the hardships and fear of living under occupation. We see her off with tears each time and we longingly wait for her return. There was no way of knowing what could happen before her next planned visit. The occupying army would often forbid the boat from sailing for any reason they would choose. Vlaho is particularly homesick. He wants to go to Orašac with his Granny on more than one occasion, but we stop him. He is to too proud to withstand the malice and provocative questioning of the interrogators in Zaton who await every new passenger and take him to their command post for questioning. He has grown to love his homeland, as he loves his parents and friends, and he particularly loves the Croatian Army. He hates all violence, so we stop him from going. He is honest and very fair.

We can see the hill on the west side of Orašac from our hotel balcony. It is quite tall, so it can be clearly seen. We cast glances towards it many times, sighing. Can it be that our home is so close, yet so far away?

It is possible for me to get a permit and take a boat to Zaton, which would enable me to go on foot to Orašac. This is, however, out of the question. My husband is a member of the Croatian Army reserve, so any type of questioning is out of the cards for me. I have formed a firm decision in my mind not to go there until our village is free one day. Our lives are spent in expectation of daily boats from Zaton, so we could ask the people arriving from those parts about the situation. We are ever fearful something bad would happen. My mother in law has fallen ill, so she comes to the doctor's quite often. She has lost a lot of weight because of her sickness. But also because of the constant fear she lives in. Sometimes in the beginning of March I have a strange dream. In it, I am walking up the stairs leading to our house, and I am crying bitterly. All around me there are carnations in full bloom. The next day the same dream occurs, only the flowers have changed; this time they are gladioli. Something is telling me, I interpret, that we will be going home exactly when carnations and irises are in bloom. I tell my husband of my dream and he tells me he hopes I am wrong because if we stay that long, he is bound to go crazy. We are all hoping that this filthy war will be over much sooner.

Days go by, and the spring is here. Ivana and her kindergarten group have a little recital. The children have prepared beautiful poems on spring, but the smiles on the faces of audience as they recite are fake. Easter is fast approaching and freedom is nowhere to be seen.

Clothes are occasionally handed by the Red Cross in the hotel. First, you have to take a number and then wait for your turn to get some second hand clothes. Vlaho is usually the one to take the number for our room. Our numbers are at the end of the line, as if by rule, and this usually means that everything worth considering has already been taken. Still, Vlaho is patiently waiting in line, and as our number comes up he runs to get me: "Mommy, Mommy, it's our turn, come quickly." He is always so cheerful. I go with him to please him, rarely finding anything to suit him or his sister. Every time he tries very hard to find something for his sister or for his parents. It gives him great pleasure.

We have borrowed the bed linen from my husband's aunt, and we take it to her place to get it washed. The hotel has not given us even that, saying that they are out, that there is too many of us.

Easter finds us still in the hotel. I dye the eggs for the children in an old tin can on the balcony. I cut some paper eggs and use crayons to color them. Afterwards I pin them to the curtain, creating at least some Easter setting for us. The Red Cross is handing packages for Easter. Only children seven years old or younger are entitled to it. I ponder the unfairness of it al as I look at my son's sad face as he patiently waits at the Red Cross doors. The age limit would be acceptable, had we not seen some older children, even ten year olds, carrying packages. As long as there is humanity, injustice is bound to follow. My heart breaks for my boy, but I tell him that his sister will share hers with him.

We spend Easter all alone; none of our relatives who live in the city has remembered to even call and ask how we are doing. W are disappointed and pretty angry with all of our relatives. My parents, being refugees themselves, are the only family that occasionally comes to visit. All those who are still in their own homes, no matter the war, cannot begin to understand the sadness of the situation we are in.

I take the children to the hotel for Easter Mass and my husband goes to the Old Town, to the Cathedral. We rarely allow the children to venture far in case there is an attack. We plan to go to town for Mass next Sunday, if it is still quite. This plan goes to waste; we are apparently not allowed to make any plans. Vlaho has a fever again. I feel sorry for him, being angry at the same time. "Is there a single sickness that passes you by!", I shout, "I'll go mad over your health."

He is quiet, not knowing what to say, lying in bed and fighting off fever. I sit with him all day long, having taken sick leave from work. His temperature is very high, and I am worried. Having nothing to make the wraps for him, I tear my undershirt into four pieces. I soak these in alcohol water and wrap them around his wrists and calves. This happens two days before White Sunday. My husband insists that I go to Mass to the town with him. I protest, not wanting to leave a sick child, but in the end I give in and go. I barely pay attention to an hour long Mass.

Ivana is left with her sick brother and I have asked my aunt to keep an eye on them. The Mass is hardly over and I leap across Stradun, run into the pharmacy to get an antibiotic and then quickly jump onto the bus. I rush into the room, worried sick for my son. He lies in bed perfectly still, a bit flushed in the face, his sister at his side. When I ask him how he is feeling, he responds briefly that he is well. I give him the antibiotic and make him eat some home made soup. He eats very little. He is sick for a whole week. The hotel children, his little friends, often come knocking on our door, wondering if their little friend is well enough to come out and play. These short visits bring him great joy; I know he wishes he were well enough to join them.

Finally, he gets well enough to go to school. He is very eager, even though he is visibly weak. After a few days Ivana gets sick. I feel I am about to break any minute. She has a very high fever, and she has only been sick a few times in her life. I take her to the Red Cross doctor who comes to the hotel once a week. She has to get some shots. The nurse does not come to the hotel regularly, so I have to take my sick girl across town to the health centre for eight whole days. They both have to have their blood tested. The results show streptococci and they are already in the blood stream. The situation is quite alarming, especially at a time like this. I think to myself: "Dear God, do we need more misery in our life? Isn't the hand we're dealt rich enough?" We are constantly forced to brace ourselves for more, and more, and more. Right about this time, the electricity and water start doing their on-off routine again. Once again we have to get used to candles, darkness and the countless buckets of sea water that are hurled up three flights of stairs. The only blessing is the fact that I do not have to go to work when the power is out. A colleague of mine has given me a bottle of cooking gas which came in more than handy during Vlaho's sickness.

Easter is near, and the semester is over for schoolchildren. Vlaho comes from school carrying his report card. He hands it to me, saying nothing. I am really impressed; he excelled in every single subject, as usually. I start kissing him and saying how proud I am. And I really am very proud of my son. It has always been a true pleasure to talk to any of his teachers.

All through April, the alarms are sounded occasionally. As much as we have all gotten used to the dreaded alarms, they still paralyze me. Our usual procedure is to go to my cousin's room; it is safer, being a floor below. We would squat between in the bathroom hallway and listen to the news intensely. I do not let the children move a single inch. One night the sirens start howling at 11. The children are sleeping and we have just gone to bed. The silence and the illusion of peace are gone; that awful, piercing sound always manages to do that. I wake the children in haste and we run to my cousin's. We sit in our improvised shelter and wait for whatever is going to happen. The children's heads are nodding; they have not even woken up yet. At two o'clock in the morning we decide to go back to our room since nothing has happened. We sleep with our clothes on in case we have to leave the room in haste. I hate the great big screen door leading to the balcony because it makes us all so exposed and vulnerable. We sleep dressed for a few days. Fear and panic are slowly creeping in again. The children are not allowed to set foot outside the hotel.

One night a powerful explosion is heard. I leap from bed, grab my son and bring him to our bed. His bed is right in front of the window. Upon returning from the balcony, my husband finds out that his place has been taken. "You're faster than a lightning!", he jokes, "And where am I supposed to sleep?" He ends up sleeping in Vlaho's bed which is particularly uncomfortable for a full grown man. In the morning we find that no grenades have been dropped, and in the end, that is what matters. We often lie half awake in bed, listening to the sounds and echoes of detonations from other neighborhoods. In case anything happens, one must react very fast. The southern wind, which is very common this time of year, is not helping us fall asleep one bit. The waves would roll the pebbles on the hotel beach in a very loud and annoying fashion all night long. The racket alone is enough to get us in a twist, and we are also, at moments like this, more than a bit mad with the people who are sleeping blissfully because their rooms do not overlook the sea. Our nerves have thinned to near nothing.

The days are getting longer, warmer and sunnier. The children are happy to be able to spend some time in the fresh air. On Sundays, if the day was sunny and, most of all, peaceful, we would take the children for a walk in the cove. Lots of people are out catching some sun, mostly refugees. I always fear that some sudden danger is going to jump at us. One day we go a bit further. Sun is shining and it is warm. We all enjoy the silence very much. As we are walking up the street past hotel Kompas, we watch men and women doing all sorts of little everyday chores in their gardens. We all hurt inside when we remember our home and start thinking of what we have been reduced to. Vlaho always wants to stay near the hotel to play with his friends, but we will not hear of it. We are still very jumpy because the war is still raging. As we walk I look for any sort of a spring flower along the road, hoping it would cheer the room a bit. Apparently, I am not the only one. People have picked all the little flowers, trying to lift their spirits at least a little bit. Vlaho occasionally finds a humble daisy or a primrose and he brings it to me happily for our little vase.

Come May, everything is fresh and green. Our longing for home becomes almost unbearable, it eats us inside. Sometimes I catch myself thinking I would never see my home again. During the whole time of our exile the children and I have only cried very, very rarely. Hope that every war must end would always suppress the tears. We live, basically, for tomorrow, for the justice that has to triumph some day; it is bound to. The spring draws the children to the near by meadows and to the beach. I keep my son on a "tight leash", he is allowed to venture only some thirty yards from the hotel. I see him looking sadly after his friends, but he is not allowed to go as far as they are. The fear rules supreme in me and I want to have him within eyesight at all times. I prefer the rain when the children are forced to stay in. During one of our Sunday walks Vlaho runs of to buy himself an ice cream cone. He has saved what little money we gave him for Christmas just for an occasion like this. Of course, now Ivana wants one. Just as I am about to go buy it for her, Vlaho appears, carrying two cones. He bought them out of his own humble allowance and he hands the rest of the money to me. I am amazed and exhilarated at these little streaks of nobility and selflessness he exhibits. They seem to come so naturally to him.

He likes to listen to the radio program for our soldiers on the front. I often have to remind him to keep it down; the people next door have recently lost their son so tragically. The painful wails of the bereaved mother would keep us up on nights without end. He does what he is told, even though he does not necessarily like it. One sunny afternoon he comes to our door glowing with happiness and pride. In his hand he carries a bunch of wild asparagus. He had hoped to cheer us all up. We get angry, out of fear, more than anything else; the hotel is practically surrounded by mine fields. We make him promise us he will never venture into the woods again. He gives us the asparagus and promises not to. My heart is breaking, we understand his point of view, but we cannot afford to be sentimental. Safety has to come first, and these are not safe times.

The month of May is, by tradition immemorial, dedicated to the Virgin Mary. The most popular devotion is, of course, the Rosary. As soon as he had noticed some people praying in one of the lounges, my son wants to go and pray with them. This surprises me greatly. The group praying consists mainly of women, many of them elderly, so it has never crossed my mind that he would be interested. I let him go, of course, and he goes to prayer quite often in the evenings. He stands by the women and listens to every word attentively.

One afternoon, after our walk, Vlaho is very hungry. He goes to get himself one of the baloney sandwiches which are a recent addition to the dinner menu. Two hours after he has eaten it he complains of a piercing pain in his tummy. He starts to convulse and throw up. He would tell me often enough that he had seen flies walk all over the sandwiches, but I took this to be a childish exaggeration. I have seen with my own eyes mice running around the kitchen and restaurant area but, as we are frequently reminded, we are not tourists and are not in a position to complain. I put him on a strict regime, hoping that the upset stomach is just a passing thing. The next day he is even worse. He cannot even keep the tea and double-baked bread in. my cousin has a car, so we rush him to the hospital immediately. The doctor gives us some saline for him to drink and puts him on a strict diet, consisting of salted pretzels and coke. We head to the pharmacy to buy the medicine, and afterwards go on a quest of finding coke in a war torn, besieged city. After a fair bit of cruising, miraculously, we manage to find it. Vlaho is exhausted and cannot wait to get into bed. I do exactly as the doctor has ordered, but it is no good. He is still very sick; if anything, I think his condition has worsened. Not eating for four days has drained his already weakened little body. It would be so much easier were it not for the constant convulsions.

By evening the situation has gotten much more serious. I fear for my son's life and I run to my cousin's room with tears in my eyes. "Vlaho is very sick;" I tell him, all panicky, "Please lend us the car so we can get him to the hospital!"

We get to the hospital at about 8:30. Ivana is left alone in the hotel room. I have forgotten all about her in all that commotion; I have not even told anybody to check in on her. The doctor asks for an immediate blood test. He asks me to take the child's shirt off. I help him out of his shirt and I break in tears seeing his torso, just skin and bones. I sit on some steps next to the hospital bed and I cry bitterly, not caring about hiding my tears. The pain that this feeling of helplessness, of not being able to help my poor, sick child, causes me is overpowering; I do not even see the doctor and the nurse standing next to me and I do not care. His father does not cry, but he aches silently in his heart when he sees his little boy in such agony.

He begs us not to leave him in the hospital. Going to the hospital was one of my more common threats when dealing with likes or dislikes concerning food in the past. I try to console him, telling him we would not leave him there, but I am aware that it is very likely we will be asked to do just that. In an hour or so the tests have all been completed. In the meantime, I remember my daughter, left alone in the room in the midst of all that commotion. I can barely stand the pounding pain searing through my head and I am actually certain I am going to loose my mind tonight. Fortunately, the results are not bad. A strict diet is the only thing to do. He got some salt for dehydration. I have to dissolve it in water and give him a teaspoon every minute. He cannot even have tea until tomorrow. The doctor asks us are we able to ensure a proper diet for our son living in a hotel. After two or free days of rigorous diet we are supposed to feed him clear veal soup and only boiled tender veal and chicken. We agree to anything to keep Vlaho from staying in the hospital. He looks at us. The tired look in his eyes is begging us not to leave him here. My mind starts hurting indescribably; I feel the pain literally tearing me apart inside.

I get him dressed and gently take him by the hand to the car. We get to the hotel at well past ten. My aunt has taken care of her and she is still up and awake. She would not go to sleep until we got back. I prepare the salt and I give it to my tormented and exhausted son each minute for an hour and a half. The next day I give him a very small piece of double-baked bread and some tea. My heart just aches as I watch my sweet, smart boy suffer. Why must he be sick al the time? Vlaho is too weak to get out of bed for the next two or three days.

A friend of ours helps us get a refrigerator. We are not allowed to have many things in the hotel, but I honestly think that our son's life is far more important than their rules. We are just ordinary, war-tired people, not tourists. I buy some veal and make my son a soup. He eats very little. The fact that I can now put a little soup in the fridge for him to eat tomorrow makes me so happy. The kitchen food is out of question. The hotel makes soup once every three weeks, and even then it is, too say the least, not very hearty. Vlaho gets used to this food regime very quickly. We eat the fish, he eats his clear soup. We eat, oranges and he is only allowed to have pureed apple. Hi is also not supposed to drink milk for a long while, only dark tea.

The cherries start to ripen. I feel terrible for my son, who can only look at them longingly in the hands of other children, but he cannot have one himself. I am constantly reminding him not to eat anything that is not on the list. When he has gotten well enough, I take him to eat with us in the restaurant for the first time. We are having chopped liver with a side of canned peas. It is hideous and I cannot force myself to eat any. Children try and take a little before giving up. Vlaho, of course, starts throwing up in a couple of hours. I get really scared and I start hating myself for allowing him to eat that repulsive meal. This is the first time since he got sick that I do not have any veal soup in the room. He has to go back to his strict regime. I am not happy to see him long for fruit and sweets while I can only feed him the diet menu, but, thank God, he is so well disciplined. I have to start preparing him his own food again. Some of his friends come asking for him in the afternoon, but I do not let him go to the restaurant to have tea wit them. The tea is left over from breakfast. They just warm it up. And, on top of everything else, I know how filthy the cups are. I have to ban a lot of things to keep him safe.

In the next few days we are back again to carrying endless buckets of sea water and having to live in a candle lit semi-darkness. There is a cherry tree growing in the hotel yard. The cherries have just started turning red and ripe, but the people whose rooms overlook the tree consider it their own. Hotel children often stop by to have a few of the newly ripened fruit. That is when the shouting and yelling start. I cannot believe that people can stoop to such primitivism. The children are, naturally, persistent, so the yelling becomes something of a regular occurrence. One day two young men come with a big bag, get up in the tree and pick about five pounds of cherries. They get the children around and they all wait their turn patiently to get a handful of cherries. I watch this moving display of humanity in the midst of war and chaos. I have to say, those boys are really great, making it possible for the kids to at least have a few cherries each. I see my son standing with the other children. I rush to the yard and take him out of the line. He was waiting for cherries he is not allowed to eat. His voice is sad as he informs me: "I am waiting in line for my sister. I know I can't eat them." Another stab in my heart; I have robbed him of that small pleasure.

As the weather got nicer, my cousins would go fishing, taking my husband with them. They evacuated from home in their boat and now it comes in handy for fishing. They usually return with a nice catch. We often grill the fish on an open fire on the beach. The rich smell of fish always takes us back to the good old days when there was no war. Vlaho is, of course, not allowed to have fish. Sometimes they would catch a lot of fish, and then Tonći would take it to the fish-market. Some of it is given to friends; it feels good to be able to give again.

Since I have to go to work, Vlaho, even though he is still pretty sick, takes his sister to the kindergarten and then goes to school. I have to cook him special meals all the time, because none of the meals coming from the kitchen is even close to the ones on his list. Their menu consists of minced chicken casseroles, pasta with that same minced meat, frozen breaded fish sticks, some hard-to-identify sausages with beans... Weekly menu is repeated endlessly, so that the day of the week can be identified by the smell coming form the kitchen. Our room has become a little crowded with things. We have stuffed boxes under the beds filled with our old refugee blankets, shoes and clothes we are not wearing any more. And we are badly wanting for space. Several of our relatives and friends have sent us parcels from abroad. The children are so happy each time a package arrives. Our winter clothes and our summer clothes are a bit too much for such a small space.

The sirens start hollering one morning while I am at work. We all have to leave our office building and go to the shelter which is located at a basement of a nearby building. The shelter is fully equipped; I notice bunk beds and gas lights, as well as a supply of drinking water. I feel panic building up inside me. My children are all alone in the hotel and I cannot get to them. We stand in the semi-darkness of the room, all of us scared and worried, and we just wait. Hours go by but no alarm is sounded to mark the end of danger. I get very restless; I just have to be with my children! There is no way for me to get in touch with them. I am going to go to my children on foot. I realize I have to take this dangerous step, because I will go insane if I have to wait another minute. I am joined by a colleague, a woman from Zaton who has found refuge in a hotel not far from ours.

We pace swiftly, eager to join our families. The silent streets are dreadful. We barely speak a few words to each other on the road. My whole body is on the alert for any kind of sound. We take some shortcuts to hasten our journey. The air is filled with danger. I check each house we pass for possible shelter, in case the attack starts. I have to walk a mile and a half to get to the hotel. We pick up our pace as we leap in utter panic to our goal. A police car drives by relatively close to us, but they do not notice us. The road ahead is clear, so we can walk straight down the middle of the driveway. We part at a crossroads after saying goodbye and wishing each other good luck.

The fear is becoming unbearable. My legs do not listen to me any more, but my heart is set on getting to my children. I muster all my courage and head on. My breath has shortened drastically due to all the effort I put in my walking. Minutes seem like hours. Grenade halls all along the road make me even more scared. Just three hundred more yards, I think to myself, and I gather all my forces as I walk. All the suspense is making me dizzy and I feel like I am going to collapse any minute. I arrive at the hotel unharmed, crying as I hug my scared children who were safe all along.

Sometime around this day, they have put a stop to boat traffic to and from Zaton. My mother in law can visit us no more. Once again, we have lost touch with her. Fear and panic are back. All schools have been closed. There is no water again, so the schools have to close for sanitary reasons, as well as the alarms that were sounded. Power is also out. Vlaho is trying to catch a crab down at the beach, and Ivana is playing with some girls in the hotel yard. I check on them frequently from our balcony.

On 25th May 1992, just when we think all hell is breaking we hear the news that the Yugoslav Army has withdrawn from the western part of the occupied territory around Dubrovnik. Our happiness cannot be described. The very next day they withdraw completely from Mokošica, Žarkovica, Dubac, Strinčjera and Bosanka.

On the 27th the enemy is pushed out of a large part of Župa, just to the east of the city. The brass band is out on the streets, playing. They walk by us in their dress uniforms, celebrating the liberation of at least a part of the occupied territory. Our hearts leap with joy. We will soon be going home to enjoy the long awaited freedom. People from Konavle still have to wait for that moment. My husband runs all the way to the harbor, wanting to know how he can get home to Orašac. He returns smiling, saying that the next boat for Zaton leaves on 28th.

All excited and worked up, he decides to take that very first boat home. He goes off to buy some meat, bread and some other things for his mother. We decide to wait in the hotel while he goes and checks out the situation. Who knows what has the enemy left behind?

The next day Tonći returns to us carrying a basket full of delicious ripe cherries and fresh spring lettuce from our garden. His mother is OK, though she has aged rapidly and noticeably.

We are thrilled with all the good news, but our good spirits are not meant to last. Just as we sat down to eat, an alarm is sounded. We eat in the room, as always, and we think that the alarm is sounded just as a precautionary measure. All of a sudden, my cousin's wife comes bursting at our door. "What are you doing here?", she shouts, "The city is under attack! Don't you listen to the radio?" Cold shivers are going down my spine as I grab the children, our documents and some of the food we kept just for cases like this. For the first time since we came to the hotel we are going down to the shelter. The underground rooms are cold and stuffy, furnished with cots and some plastic chairs. Only the more power-ful radios can get any signal. The attack underway is fierce. When-ever the door to the shelter slam, be it from the wind or because some child has slammed into it, we think that it is the grenade. We sit in there for about three hours, having lost any clue as to what is happening outside. Many of us are in the shelter. The braver ones have stayed in the hotel corridors, saying they feel safe right there. No sound can be made out, the wind howling and the screeching of doors makes it impossible. Later on we learn that a few of the grenades have indeed landed near us. Several hours later, after we have frozen completely, we get out of the shelter and go to my cousin's room, it being safer than ours. We sit on the floor, and the children silently climb onto a bed. The night is falling and we have fallen once again to fear and panic. We spend the night fully dressed and dozing. The first crack of dawn brings us a sense of relief.

The attacks continue; the city blocks are attacked most fierce-ly. Nineteen people were wounded that day. Our first refugee home, uncle's house, has been hit. I feel a sense of great relief that we were not there to experience the shock. At the same time I am profoundly sorry for the people who gave us shelter during those first months of war. Luckily, no one was hurt.

We spend most of the day in a stuffy shelter, scared and con-fused. We thought we were free! Attacks continue every day until 6th June. Detonations blast all through the days, but at least the nights are quiet. The children are not allowed to meet in the hall-ways while this is going on. The top floor corridor has huge sky-lights which puts us in even more danger. The food is distributed swiftly in the kitchen. Since the alarm was first sounded, the hotel staff has halved, so younger people from the hotel helped with the chores. The power has gone out again, couple of days after we fi-nally got it. We all know what this means: more buckets of water and more candles.

We pass time by playing chess and listening to the news. We spend endless hours theorizing about the war and ways to end it. Vlaho and Ivana are behaving great, even though I myself am not sure why they are not allowed to at least take a stroll down a hotel corridor.

The ferry starts to sail for Zaton sometime around these days. It serves as a military transport and sets sail several times a day. They take on civilian passengers who have the proper permits from the Civil Guard officials. We were not aware of the need for such permits, so we cannot board and sail home. Looking for an alternative way, we find a man who is going to Štikovica by his own boat. We make all the arrangements. The next day we are supposed to sail, and it is raining heavily, so we have to cancel. We cannot accept this, so Tonći wanders off, looking for other ways.

On 8th June he arrives happily at two o'clock, waving a piece of paper. "We can go home for a whole week. I have the permit!" I am immensely happy. He wants to go that same afternoon, at six. I try to put it off for tomorrow, as I fear a sudden attack. He insists on leaving today. The alarm which was sounded on 29th May is still on.

The day is cloudy. I pack a few necessary things for us to take. The children are besides themselves with joy. They were very disappointed two days ago, when rain interfered with pour plans. We buy some food, bread and other things, pack it al and start on foot towards the harbor at 4:45. Vlaho carries his school books, Tonći and I some clothes and food. Ivana carries her doll, as we walk, I am afraid of the attack and still wonder about the decision to leave while the alarm is still on, quickly and in silence. The ferry takes no heed of the status of alert. I ask my son if his beg is too heavy, but he refuses assistance. He is still very thin and pale from all the throwing up and dieting. The journey is very long, each step made harder by all the things we are carrying, while trying to make haste. We have to stop every now and then to catch our breath.

When we finally reach the harbor, our hearts begin to race. Can it really be that we are going home after eight months of exile?

My dream has indeed come true. At the harbor gate I notice some carnations in full bloom. We arrived at the pier at 5:30, and the minutes leading up to 6 are ever so slow. The fear of a possible attack is still present. We are eager to get on the ferry. Everyone carries a lot of luggage; it is a proper migration. Ten minutes before the departure, we are allowed to board. I read the ferry's name, "Zamošće", and I remember it well.

At six o'clock the ferry departs. A strange feeling, impossible to describe, starts to flood my whole being. It starts to rain, so I take the children inside the onboard restaurant. I see many familiar faces. They too are coming home for the first time.

The rain stops as we approach Zaton. I go to deck to see the sailing in at the exact place we have left eight months ago in panic. I take the children up on deck, wanting them to feel this glorious moment of homecoming and to remember it always. I make a mental note to sit down and document this whole ordeal that befell us during the war and exile from home for them to know. I want to ensure their memory, even at an older age, when memories of detail are bound to fade. The afternoon sun starts shining on us and on the pier we are approaching. The site is unforgettable. I hold back the tears, but my throat is completely clenched. Can it be, could I be dreaming, we are home! The ferry slowly approaches the pier and people get restless, wanting to get off. The engines start turning off and everyone charges on the exit. The ferry is also loaded with cars, whose owners are also anxious to leave. The Zaton pier is loaded with people, smiling and crying at the same time. Lots of them are waiting for their loved ones. The road is still closed, partly under enemy control, so the ferry is the only way in or out. We run into a man we know on the ferry, and he agrees to drive us home in his car. This last phase of our homeward journey seems like a dream. Is this really the same road we ran on, so unhappy, towards the Town? We greet some of the neighbors on the way and hurry on home. Carnations are everywhere. I feel so strange. I thought that I would cry with happiness once I return home, but there are no tears. Just a strange weight pressing my chest. The house is locked. We find the key in its old hiding place. As I enter the house, it seems like a castle to my eyes. Having been forced to live in a single room for so long, we are able to fully soak in the luxury and comfort of our home. Mother is in the garden, behind the house. She is radiant with happiness as she comes in, hugging and kissing all of us. For the first time in eight months we sit and dine at our own table. We sit and talk for a long time. Mother slept in the new house during these days of war. The house is only partly furnished, but it is solidly built, and everything else gives place to safety during the war. We are excited enjoying the fact that tonight we are going to sleep in our own home after such a long time. We wake up early, thrilled by the fact that our refugee days are finally over. The very thought of the hotel repulses me. We will finally eat normal food again. Since there is no power the fridge is of no use to us. Besides, meat has become something of a luxury these days. We ate fresh vegetables, eggs, fish, cheese and milk. There is a supply of beans of all sorts and a few humanitarian aid cans. I make a roast chicken on Sunday. Every little thing makes us so happy. We use the old wood stove to prepare bread.

The children miss all their friends from the hotel. Since we left in somewhat of a hurry, they have not had the chance to say goodbye to anyone. Our permit states that we have to go back, if only for a short while, so they brighten up a bit. The warmth and beauty of our home make us forget all about the gray coldness of hotel living.

13th June is approaching, the feast day of Saint Anthony, my husband's patron saint. We have been to town the day before. We wanted to prepare a little feast, to join the feast day celebration with our homecoming. We bought some meat and a few things we missed. We also went to the hotel to collect some more things and say goodbye to our friends and family. All the time I keep thinking how we have learned to think of that small hotel room as our home. After all, it was exactly that for almost six months. I still feel much safer when the ferry takes off and sets sail toward Zaton. As if we were sailing to a safe haven.

A Croatian Army artillery battery has been firing from our village for days. The whole village is shaking with the force of the cannon. There is no alarm system, so every time a new explosion sounds, I jump with fear. It was louder than loud. A dog from Osojnik found refuge in our village. His name is Tabo and he is awfully afraid of the sound of gunfire. Whenever a blast is heard, he hides between the two walls in front of our house and lies there for hours, even after the gun fire has long stopped.

During one of the attacks the forest above the houses starts burning. We all run to help put out the fire. Suddenly, I realize that my son is standing next to me, trying to stomp the fire with a branch. I have a hard time convincing him to go home because it is not safe for him to be here.

People have already started going about their own business. Grenades often fly over us, their whistling raising the fine hair on our necks. Summer has started, so we usually eat both lunch and dinner on the terrace. We were not the frontline any more, but when a hissing and a whistling are heard, we go to the house with the children, just to be on the safe side.

Upon his return home, Vlaho made a thorough inspection. He drew a great big Croatian flag and put it at the entrance to our front yard. He even said hi to our old goat. We knew this by his face – he swells up from his allergy to animal hair. He runs to check in on the hens and comes out with eggs in his hands. The old wheelbarrow is making a lot of noise around the house. It has been silent for too long. The wheelbarrow is one of Vlaho's favorite "toys". He loves pushing his sister in it around the house. He has also fixed the old barn doors that have come loose.

When the shooting has quieted down, I go to Kodo one day. We have land there, some planted with vine, some with olives and some with cherry trees. I am very sad when I see the old quince has not made it. Vlaho loves the jam I made from its fruit. A few steps from the old tree everything was burned. The blackberry bushes I used to pick as a child were gone. The sadness I feel will pass, I know that; our home is intact, thanks to Granny, and our lives are the most precious. Granny has told us that the enemy soldiers have ransacked both houses before they left. They kept asking her to surrender the weapons they knew she did not have. My husband had hid his hunting rifle before we left, and had buried our jewelry and documents. Not having found the weapons, the soldiers took al of Granny's money, smoked hams and her few pieces of jewelry. They also took humanitarian aid cans and Vlaho's toy gun. Vlaho was sad to hear this, but his dad promised to buy him another for Christmas. On returning home Vlaho made friends with the "Tigers". They are a brigade of volunteers who have come to help liberate our home. They moved into an empty house not far from us, so Vlaho practically lives there. He was very proud when they gave him a camouflage shirt and a badge. Later on, when they add a hat to this, he is beside himself. We often send him over to their house with some cheese or homemade wine.

My sister comes to visit with her husband. We hold each other after a full year. Tears stream down both our faces. The most important thing is that they are all right, too. My sister in law arrives on the afternoon ferry that same day. They have been refugees, too. They are coming to stay for a couple of days, until they can move into their own apartment in Mokošica.

The attacks on the city itself have increased in frequency in the meantime. They stay with us, so there are nine of us in the house now. There is plenty of food and space, so we do not worry. We listen to the news every evening and we are grateful that we are out of the city. It seems so much more dangerous there. Vlaho and Ivana now have their cousins to play with, and the adults share the workload. Water has to be fetched from the well, and we cook on gas. All laundry and linen is done the old-fashioned way.

My husband and I often go to our old hotel room. We wish to take the rest of our things with us. We ask for our room to be left vacant for just a little while, because we have no means by which to transport all of our belongings at once. Officially, we are not even allowed to return to Orašac yet. Each time we go to town our son asks to go with us so he can say goodbye to his friends. We refuse every time, because we consider the city area to be too dangerous. He cannot wait for things to get better, so he could go. Sirens are often heard from the city. We only go to town if there is no alert sounded, even though detonations can always be heard echoing from a distance. The children have slowly adapted to being back at home, and they do not even mention the hotel or their friends any more. Vlaho spends a lot of time with his soldier friends the day is relatively quiet, so I go to pick some vegetables in the field. The second after I arrived, grenades start whooshing over my head. They flew over us to explode not far from the place I was standing at. I stop for a minute. The hissing is dreadful and I start running towards home, some three hundred yards away. My husband is often on the tractor this time of day, and he sometimes narrowly escapes.

At the beginning of July, while we are still sleeping, around five in the morning, I am awakened by a strange noise. The children are sleeping in their room. I wonder what sort of a new weapon the sound belongs to. The sound repeats and suddenly, we hear a neighbor shout: "Planes!" I jump out of bed as fast as I can, wake the children and take them to the ground floor. I place them into a corner I feel is the safest place to be. Ivana is scared; she sits quietly on her chair wrapped in a blanket. Vlaho is wrapped in a blanket, too, but he complains about having been woken up. He wants to go to his room. He tells me, as he usually does: "You know they won't hurt me, Mommy!" I get a little angry with him, but as the planes are no longer heard, eventually I let him go to his room. He sleeps in a room that faces the sea, and shares the eastern wall with an empty room, so it is relatively safe. He fears nothing, even though he has lived through the fears of bombs and grenades during our months in the city. Later on we learn that the planes we have heard were in fact Croatian war planes. They have flown over very low and bombed the enemy stronghold over the river Ombla, the notorious sniper nest on a rock high in the hills.

The sirens go off very often in the city. Some of our things are still in the hotel. The ferry does not take civilian cars during the alert. The lines are very long if we are to go by car, anyway. The road is still closed, so this is the only link between the city and these several villages. One day we have to wait for hours, and cannot embark in the end. There is only room for passengers. The other time we take Vlaho's bike with us and attach some bags containing our things from the hotel. I carry the rest in my arms, so we manage to transport the bulk of our refugee property. The children in the hotel always ask of Vlaho and Ivana. The boys particularly miss Vlaho.

On 2nd July, the feast day of Our Lady of Orašac, I go to church barefoot, as I have vowed I would. Regardless of danger, a large number of people rush to church which is, as if by miracle, completely untouched by the hand of the enemy.

7th July. It is raining slightly. It is unusually cold and rainy for this time of the year. The day is quiet, so we decide to take our small car to the hotel and move the rest of our things out of there. The car has to be assembled first, of course, because my husband has taken it apart before we left so it would not be stolen. In Zaton we are told that we cannot board the ferry any more. We can, if we wish to, take the road which has been in unofficial use for the last two days. We are not sure whether to take the still insecure road.

It is finally open after nearly nine months. The greatest danger comes from Golubov kamen, a sniper nest in the hills overlooking the road. It is supposed to be free, the enemy driven away. We decide to take our chances and we take the road. Driving in silence, we approach the Ombla River. We are faced with the first images of destruction and burnt houses in Mokošica. The fear is growing inside me as we are nearing Rožat and the bridge across the river. What if things suddenly change? Are we going to be lucky enough to pass this, the most dangerous, section of the road safely? Our car is screaming, driving at the highest gear, and we feel like it is barely moving. The gas station at Komolac is literally leveled and all the houses around it are burned. We sigh with relief as we get to Sustjepan. God has watched over us, and we have placed most of our hope with the fog that was enveloping the sniper rock, making the passage safe. We arrive at the hotel at two o'clock and pack the rest of the things quickly. I clean the room and wash the bathroom. All that is left is to return the key at the front desk and we are rid of the refugee room and all the bed memories.

The skies clear in the afternoon and we want to go back as soon as possible. The evenings are almost never quiet. The luck is once again on our side and we get home safely at about six. I feel a great relief that it is all behind us. We hear the detonations only an hour later. The Ombla River area is being bombed.

There is talk of the electricity being on its way. First, the damaged power lines leading through Primorje have to be repaired. I am not happy about the power, because that would mean going back to work. This is a very difficult feat to accomplish from Orašac, even though some of those working in hotels or stores are forced to undertake it. I am also worried about the possibility of getting caught in the alert while in city, and this would mean going to the first shelter and being away from my family.

We have gotten used to living modestly. There are still nine of us in the house. The days are starting to get very hot, and we have to use the wood stove and cooker. We sweat heavily over it, and remember the nicer times, when we used to live the lives of civilized people. We tough it out, always remembering that this is so much easier than those months spent in the hotel. The children from Orašac go to swim, but we do not allow our son to venture to the sea. After his fervent pleas, we allow it, but only under the condition that they are accompanied by an adult. Sometimes, we also go. He is overjoyed to be able to go swimming for an hour or two. He is always home on time.

The Croatian Army is stationed at the tourist apartment complex not far from us. The luxurious and richly decorated facilities were completely pillaged by the Yugoslav soldiers. Everything except the very walls has been taken. The Croatian soldiers now living there come from all parts of Croatia. We have relatives in Split, and since the phone lines are dead my husband's uncle has asked a soldier to ask around for information of us. The man has found us and we have met his two friends as well. He asks Vlaho what he wants the soldiers to bring him the next time they come to visit. Vlaho wants a backpack for school, an army one. The soldiers promise to try, and the next time they come they hand the backpack to Vlaho who is very happy. His school bag is too old, and these military backpacks are very popular with boys in school. He carries it around on his shoulders all evening.

He visits the Tigers, the soldiers living in our neighborhood, almost every day. They always give him some juice, a pudding or some chocolate. He always brings half of everything to his sister. Many children simply flock around the soldiers, but they seem to like Vlaho the most, because he is quiet and very polite. They often give him old bread for the chickens or some cans of food. He is always happy and very grateful for these small tokens of appreciation.

He is aware that food is scarce and is very glad to be able to help us. To repay such kindness we send the soldiers wine and fruit, mostly figs and grapes. The bread they give us for the chickens is never older than a day. I remember the time we were living at uncle's place; the bread we ate was always at least four days old.

One day Vlaho's sandals break. I want to give him mine, but they are too big for him. As we go to rest in the afternoon, Vlaho repairs his sandals himself. They look as good as new. He collects used bullet casings and builds things out of them. He glues them to the back of his little trucks and paints it all in camouflage, to resemble the Croatian Army trucks.

On 20th July I have to go to work. The bus-line from Pelješac starts driving daily. It starts from Pelješac early in the morning and returns in the afternoon, at two o'clock. This is the only link we have with the city since the ferry has left us and gone to Korčula to resume its regular route. The heats have started. The work is hard and the bus back is always filled to the capacity. It is used by the people from the whole area west of Dubrovnik. Most of the population has returned to their homes. Leaving home I always fear getting trapped in the city separated from the children. The phones are dead, so there is no way for me to contact them. The city has gotten water and power; we are still not that lucky. We are used to living without such things, anyway, so we do not miss them. We light the paraffin lamp every night and this minimum light is enough for us. My sister in law moves out to her own apartment by the end of July. Our family is now on its own.

One day I make pancakes for Vlaho's Tiger friends. As he is to leave I tell him to just hand it to them and return home, because I do not want them to think I expect something in return. He is back in a flash, but he has something in a nylon bag. I start shouting at him, and he starts explaining: "They asked me if I needed anything, and I told them that Mom needed candles, so they gave me four. They have a whole box, you know." My eyes fill up with tears. My boy is only nine and a half years old and he thinks of the family, not himself. He did not ask for a chocolate, or candy – he is thrilled at having gotten four candles, so our nights could be lighter. I hug and thank him.

Days are very hot and they go by in peace by now. Vlaho goes to our new acquaintances from Split to get the bread every day. They have told us not to bake bread, because they get a lot of it. It is a relief not having to bake bread in this heat. Our son, who was so thin and exhausted when we got back, is now fully recovered and has grown a bit taller. He is truly a young man now, in behavior, as well as in his looks. Our new soldier friends from Split like him a lot. They always tell us that he is so smart and bright and that he behaves like a grown man. He has learnt to love his country and the Croatian Army during the war, because he has seen the sadness and pain from which they got us out. They give him the Croatian Army badge and he puts it on the hat he was previously given.

At the beginning of August an army brigade is forced to change position. The enemy has learned of their old position in Gromača, so they requested a new one. They are now at Kodo. They have an outpost, some five hundred yards further. This duty is entrusted to the local men. Their duty is to guard the road to the artillery batteries and to the brigade. Not even the people from the neighboring village are allowed to pass, even though they always used that road up to now. They had to go all around over Gromača. It is war time, so every rule has to be obeyed. The guards have gotten used to our family. Their guard post is right at the beginning of our field. The only useful land we own is here. They have stopped us a couple of times and asked us where we were going, but they have seen that we only go as far as our field. Vlaho is very glad to have the soldiers so close to home. He enjoys going with us when we go to the field so he can spend time with those young men. The heats are great, and they are not allowed to leave their post. The mineral water they get warms up after a couple of hours.

Vlaho takes them some water from our well every morning and evening. They like him a lot, and his visits make long days at the watch post easier to bear. He talks with them for a long time and they had also taught him to fire a gun. I often protest, saying that they should not teach him things like that, but they tell me not to worry, that they are looking after him. They are amazed at the speed he picks up everything they show him, like assembling and disassembling a gun. They also tell us quite often how intelligent and well behaved they think he is. He is never too tired to carry the water to the soldiers. If they run out of cigarettes he runs to the store to buy some for them. He never skips one of his water rounds. He is an obedient child and we know where he is at all times. He always asks for our permission, especially to go visit the guard at Kodo.

Even though it has been quiet for a while, we fear letting him go there. Usually, there is at least one grown up from the family in the field. Granny would watch our two goats, I would pick figs for drying and his dad would plow the land which was not worked on for a year now. At dusk we return home, and Vlaho is with us. His laughter and cheer voice resound all around Kodo. I am curious, so I often ask him of his talks with those young men. He pretends to be very grown and keeps his talks with them to himself. Granny would often tell them to send him home if he is a nuisance. They always say that their little friend is no bother, that they like having him around to pass the time. They like him and trust him so they sometimes let him go to the brigade from Bjelovar, the one whose position they are guarding. It is located less than half a mile from the guard post. He proudly tells us of the huge tent, cannons, tanks and the soldiers he has seen there. He often marches around with a piece of wood propped on his shoulder like a gun. I am proud of my son and I like this fondness he feels for the Croatian Army. Most of his love is now directed at them.

Vlaho goes to bed early. He takes a bath at nine and wants me to tuck him in. I have to go with him because he will not go to sleep without his good night kiss. This happens every single night. He falls asleep fast because his days are filled with excitement and he is tired.

We also get the water at the beginning of August. We are glad not to be forced to carry numerous buckets of water from the well. It has gotten very hot and since it has been quite peaceful for awhile, we move to the old house. It has wooden floors, but its stone walls are about thirty inches thick. I put the children to sleep on the couch in the smaller room, but Vlaho soon moves to the hall. He is too hot sleeping with his sister, so this arrangement is better for both of them. Our soldier friend gets a few days off on 27th August, so he goes home to Split. As soon as he has gotten home, he phones us.

He asks for Vlaho. He works as a mechanic in his unit. He asks Vlaho to run to the apartment complex and look for the other mechanic. He has to tell him to tighten the brakes on one of the trucks, because our friend has forgotten to do this in hurry. Vlaho runs there right away and gives the message. He is in time to prevent a horrible accident which would doubtlessly happen had someone taken the truck.

That Wednesday, Vlaho takes a thermos of coffee and some pancakes to the soldiers at the guard post. I feel sorry for the young men standing in that heat, so I want to do something to cheer them up. He is very happy to take it to them and when he returns I tell him to get me some figs because our soldier friends will be coming to coffee. He wants to take the wheelbarrow to go to Kodo to get figs, and he can also pick up the cups and the thermos. A very steep hill path leads there and I object, because I think it will be difficult for him to push the wheelbarrow up it. He still takes the wheelbarrow and heads to the field. He is back after half an hour, sweat streaming down his body. His face and forehead are completely wet. I have never seen even a grown man sweat that much. I send him to the house to cool off a bit, as I am worried he will get sick. The next day he comes home all black – only his eyes are shining on his face. I get very angry. I ask him what has he done, he answers: "A cannon has broken down, so I helped fix it."

We have had electricity since 20th August, so the fridges are working, and the much wanted light is here. After ten and a half months life is finally getting a bit more normal. Vlaho brings home empty mineral water bottles, fills them half way up and freezes them. He pours water over the ice, so that his soldier friends can have icy cold water.

He has not gone swimming for the past ten days, so I am surprised when he asks to go with his friends that Saturday. He is back right on time. He showers on the terrace, using the garden hose. He likes this so much more than actually going to the shower. He stays home in the afternoon, playing with his friends. They all ride around on his bike, the one we gave him two years ago for doing well at school. He has not driven for a long time.

Sunday, 30th August

Vlaho gets up early, eats breakfast and goes to take water to the soldiers. He is back in an hour, takes a bath and I cut his fingernails. Surprisingly, he does not complain that it hurts, as usual. I sit on a small bench as Vlaho suddenly jumps at me and gives me a kiss. I look at him inquisitively; usually he only kisses me before going to bed. He gets mad at me if I want to kiss him in broad daylight. He gets dressed and goes to church. We all go this Sunday. Vlaho and his friend Antonio, who goes to Kodo with him to visit the soldiers quite often, are serving as altar-boys. A boy is baptized during the Mass. When we get home our son is already there, waiting for us. It is really hot, so he has taken his shirt off, basking in the sun happily. He goes to change for lunch. We have not bought chicken for Sunday, as we usually do, so I prepare some vegetable soup, open a can of spam and make a tomato salad. Vlaho eats everything without a word. War has taught us to be grateful for everything. He is extremely happy today and his eyes shine. I cannot remember seeing him so happy. He sits next to his father, across from me. After lunch, he asks his father for a little wine. He has never asked for this before. His father pours him less than a finger of wine and fills the rest of the glass with water. He drinks it up and asks for some more, but this time without water. I get angry and I tell my husband not to give it to him. After some persuasion, he gets his wine. He drinks it all and asks us if he can go visit his soldier friends. We let him go briefly, and he is back soon. He has a small chocolate in his hand – he has brought it to his sister. He plays with his friends all afternoon; he has not played for a long time. He goes looking for his school friend from the neighborhood (his name is Vlaho, too) and finds him with the Tigers, the brigade he too used to hang out with before. He gets back at a quarter to six and I ask him where he has been. "I've gone to see the Tigers," he answers, "I really wanted to see them." I am surprised at this; most of them have changed, so he really knows a few of them at best.

As I am getting ready to water the flowers, my son comes by and asks of the time. As I tell him it is seven forty-five he shouts: "I'm late! I'm late!". "Where are you late?" I ask, and he answers: "To Kodo." I tell him that his Daddy will be angry and that it is late. It will soon be dark and the dinner is almost ready. He runs into the house to get the cold water and shouts at me: "I'll be back real soon. Just this once, please?!" I yell after him: "Be sure to hurry back, before the night falls!" I boil some fresh vegetables and get out some salted sardines. We dine late, as we always do in the summer.

We sit at the terrace table right after eight waiting for Vlaho to return. I want to take a flashlight and go look for him, but something stops me. I think to myself that one of the young men is likely to bring him home.

A few minutes go by and a powerful blast is heard. Small pieces of rock shower our house and the terrace we are sitting on. "Tonći, Vlaho is not home yet!" I scream in panic, "Run! Go see where he is!" Another grenade flies over our heads that moment. I grab Ivana and we run over to our home shelter. My husband immediately runs over to Kodo, some three hundred yards from our house. As he gets close, he starts calling for our son. The soldiers tell him that they have put him on a van and taken him to Orašac. Tonći comes home frightened, but he reassures me that Vlaho is safe, the soldiers have taken him to safety. Some twenty minutes pass and Vlaho is still not coming, he has not even called. We start to have doubts. We leave Ivana with Granny. Tonći goes down to the Tigers to look for him, and I take the flashlight and head for Kodo. I call for the guards and they answer, telling me to go home. "Please, tell me, is my son alive?" I shout at them. All I hear is silence, an aching silence that tells me more than words could. That very moment I understand what has happened. The silent soldiers have told me the truth that no one dared speak out loud. I, a mother, standing alone on a goat track at Kodo, have found out that I no longer have my beloved son. Nobody has taken him to safety in a van. An enemy grenade has fallen a couple of yards behind my son and his soldier friend.

I do not know where from, but I muster enough strength to turn around and start back, alone in the dark, the heavy burden of truth weighing on my soul. From a distance I hear my husband's painful wail as it pierces the silence. I barely get to the first houses, broken with pain, in disbelief. I cannot believe my ears. People, rude and inconsiderate, are already telling each other: "Vlaho was killed!"

I want to be killed, I want to perish from this world, but nothing happens. I do not remember getting home. Even though I still do not believe it all, I scream with pain as loud as I can. Somebody takes Ivana to the neighbor's. The doctor and the nurse are called.

I refuse any sort of tranquilizer or anything that would kill my emotions. I do not want anything that will kill my pain for my son. My heart is crying, but my mind still understands nothing. They manage to give us some tranquilizers after all. The terrace is filled with people. I throw glasses from the table until someone has stopped me.

I do not know what the time when we go to bed is. All I know is that my heart screams in agony as we lock the door. For the first time ever we lock the door and Vlaho is not in the house.

The next day, my son, I call for you to get up, but you do not hear me. The house and the terrace filled with people in uniforms who knew and loved you are all that I see through my tear-filled eyes. You were precious to your soldier friends and the city defense high-command has sent a wreath with the words written on it:

LAST GOODBYE TO VLAHO
OUR YOUNGEST WARRIOR.

Vlaho and Ivo Miljević, one of the soldiers, have left the guard post about thirty yards east of the post. They wanted to check the road to see if the change of guards is on the way.

The shift was an hour late; instead of 7:30 they arrived at 8:30. It was far too late by then.

Your friends called you a little warrior because you truly did your best to help them. You were their courier of sorts, bringing them water, coffee and cigarettes. You loved Croatia, your homeland, and you loved our army. You also loved your home, the home you had to leave ten months ago and go to exile. You were only a little boy, but you were a great man; a great son of mine and a great son of Croatia!

Fiery fungus II, Dec. 1991. (photo: Pavo Urban)

FORGIVE ME, MY DAUGHTER

AT KODO

At Kodo, on the hard rock,
My son sleeps in death's embrace.
At Kodo, on the hard rock...
He left his little sister,
Left his parents,
Left his friends.
At Kodo, on the hard rock,
He left his school,
Left his favorite games,
Left his childish dreams.
At Kodo, on the hard rock,
You left your childhood.
You left everything, my son,
Even though
You never wanted to do so.

AMONG THE HEADSTONES

In the graveyard, among the headstones,
I wander, calling for my son.
In the graveyard, among the headstones,
Father is looking for his sweet boy.
Painful is the path which you trod on
So happily, that last day.
Even more painful is the one
Which we trod on,
Following you to your last resting place.
Futile are the kisses
Your father places
On the cold marble slab.
The flowers your mother presses
To her aching bosom
Hold no comfort.
What have the villains done to you?
Why did you not come back,
Our beloved son?
Cypresses sigh, reverently quiet,
A bird's cry breaks the solemn silence,
All the while our tears wash
That cold marble slab.
This is not a place for you,
Our beloved son!

SATAN

You, who have neither heart nor soul,
You, who think that you will live forever,
You have killed my son.
You have killed his body, but know!
You have not killed his soul!
You cannot know that,
You pitiful demonic soul.
Look around you,
Look at your own children,
Those dearest to you.
Think of them – do you love them?
No, you love no one,
For, if you did,
You would not be harming others.
O, Satan,
You don't even love yourself!
You are not a man.
Not even a shadow of a man!
You pitiful and miserable demonic soul.
Know and remember well,
Your end
Will come one day!
Oh, what a bitter and just truth.
Satan,
You will not last forever!

THE FIRST DAY OF SCHOOL

The school bell rings,
Clear voices chime!
The school has started,
Children run around.
All the seats are taken,
All but one.
One of the classes
Is a student short,
A diligent student,
A hard working boy.
Friends shake hands and hug,
A year apart is long.
Youthful hearts are filled with joy,
But one heart beats no more.
Many happy voices
Echo in the halls.
Only my son's voice will never
Be heard there again.

FORGIVE ME, MY SON

Forgive me, my son,
Please forgive me,
For having loved you,
And never being able
To show it fully.
Forgive me, my son
For all the harsh words
You did not deserve.
Forgive me for all
The things I have forbidden.
They were all for your own safety.
Forgive me
For all the punishments,
Forgive me for all the shouts.
I meant no harm, my son.
Mommy wanted
You to stay with us.
But fate had other plans.
It has taken you from me, my joy.
My shouts were in vain,
In vain was my watchfulness.
In vain I took you from your home,
Everything Mommy did
Was in vain.
Forgive me, my son,
For letting you stay late
That one evening.
Forgive me
For having given in
That once.
Forgive me,

For it only took that once.
Forgive me, my son,
For I am chastised enough
By the, oh, so heavy cross,
Which rests forever
On my shoulders.

THE VICTORY BELLS

Listen, my son,
The bells are ringing,
Free of all pain and toil.
They ring the sweet notes
Of victory and peace,
For all the people to rejoice.
O, Liberty! How bitter you are!
Listen, my son, my aching wound,
A bell is ringing for you!
But, alas! you are not among us
Anymore.
Tears of pain moisten my face,
I stand alone, without a single word.
Oh, God! The bells have fallen silent
Long ago.

THE RED-CROSS DOLL

Oh, how I loathe that Red-Cross doll!
It came to our home
In your stead, my son.
And nobody may, or indeed can,
Stand in your place.
It was brought to your sister
To take the place of her brother.
There isn't a doll in this world
Which could replace you
In your sister's heart.
I hate it, I hate it so much,
But I cannot say this to your sister.
She is only a little girl,
But soon she'll understand everything.
She will understand
Why she alone
Has an angel for a brother.
She will understand
Why her mother so loathes
That Red-Cross doll.

SORROW

Crushing is our sorrow,
Crushing is our pain, son.
Tearful are the eyes of your parents,
Painful are the long nights.
Your sister sits silently at the table,
Your granny prays fervently in the corner.
Mommy wipes her tears secretly,
Daddy fights off a painful sigh.
Joy has left our midst.
Our days are filled with pain,
Even more so our nights.
Where are you, son, joy of our being?
Where is the sun of our lives?
Your sister speaks of angels,
She seeks you, my son.
Your Daddy utters a cry,
He wants you, my son.
Your granny prays in the corner,
She cannot stand your absence.
Your Mommy wipes her tears, my love.
Oh, son!
Mommy will perish without you.

TO EUROPE AND AMERICA

O, Europe, curse on you,
You have killed this mother's son.
O, America, in your egoism,
You have killed my son.
Can children be defended
With sacks of flour?
Can they be defended
With sacks of rice?
Shame on you,
The great of this world,
Your souls are so small!
The innocents lie dead all around,
Mothers, fathers with their children.
Doesn't their blood move your hearts?
You are the masters of the world!
Your speech abundant with human rights,
Your hearts are black and cold.
Our land gives you no oil,
The blood of our sons is not black gold!
O, Europe! O, America!
All our blood and that of our children
Stains your hands!
O, Europe! O, America!
You were far too late!

CHRISTMAS 1992

Christmas Eve, silent and cold.
Children talk merrily of caroling.
People hurry home
To their Christmas trees.
In our home there is
No tree and no joyful carol,
No cookies, no Christmas roast,
Only pain, and sadness, too.
We don't wear our festive garb.
Christmas Eve, dark and cold.
Carol is heard, the children sing,
While tears stream down our faces.
Why are you not here, our beloved son?
Why do we not hear your merry voice?
Why don't the children
Knock on our door this night?
Silence is ominous,
Our eyes filled with tears,
And our hearts
With shattering pain.
You are not with us, beloved son,
You were ripped from us.
It's Christmas, silence covers all.
There are joy and glittering Christmas trees
Behind every window.
It's Christmas, we sit in silence,
Our table plain and simple.
Behind our window it feel like Lent,
Our faces washed with tears of pain.
Why, son? Why are you not
With us today?
"Mommy, is it Christmas?"
Your little sister asks.

AT DUSK

On a gray marble tombstone,
A single white lily rests.
Candle's golden glow
Flickers at dusk.
I stand straight and mute,
Surrendering to peace
Which envelopes my being.
I seek my soul's peace
In the whiteness of the flower!
My spirit is nourished with silence,
As my thoughts
Are surrendered to the universe.

GRAY TOMB

The gray tomb,
With its white plaque
Catches the eye from afar.
White roses
And
The smiling face
In the picture
Draw tears,
Weigh heavily on the heart.
What are you doing, child,
In that gray tomb?

EASTER 1993

Your sister asked me, my sweet son:
"Are we going to have Easter eggs?"
I don't know, daughter.
There is no dye for the eggs this year.
How then have other mommies
Dyed eggs for their children?
I told her that
They must have had
Some dye left over from last year.
"O, Mommy, why has our for taken
The redness of Easter eggs,
As well as the Yuletide trimmings?"
Forgive me, daughter,
You are still too little to know
Why there is no Christmas tree
Or Easter eggs in our home!

MY SON!

The spring has come, my son,
The spring birds have arrived.
Fields are waiting for you
In full bloom,
Your friends are waiting, too.
My arms are spread wide,
Waiting for you, my son.
Your sister waits for your embrace
And to sleep beside you
Through the night.
Daddy waits for you to help him,
Your bike for you to ride it.
Your school bag is here,
Covered with dust.
Where are you, son?
Can you not hear us?
The spring has come in vain,
The flowers make no sense.
Your sister's sighs for you
Are futile also!
Your mother spreads her arms
To no avail.
Vainly does your Daddy
Wait for you assistance.
We cannot understand
That you are no more, son!
Our love is gone,
Our spring is gone!
Our pride and joy is lost,
You are gone from this earth,
My good boy,
Gone from our lives
Never to return.

FORGIVE ME, DAUGHTER

Forgive me, daughter,
For not telling you
It is your birthday today.
So many times
You have asked:
Mommy, when is my birthday?
When the summer comes,
I would always say.
Summer has come
And your birthday, too,
And I said nothing.
I kissed you a lot,
Gently caressed your hair,
But I was not
Courageous enough to say:
Baby girl, it is your birthday today!
You'd ask for a cake,
For candles and friends,
And my heart is not ready for joy yet.
It still bleeds heavily,
I still miss my good boy
Too much,
Your big brother, my daughter.
Forgive me, my love,
Please forgive me.
Forgive me for your seventh birthday.
Have I told you then
You would never forgive me.
When you get bigger
I am sure you will
Forgive your mother

For your seventh birthday.
A candle was burning for you
On the high altar that Sunday,
It was burning with the strength
Of all my wishes for you,
For your good health and happiness.
I love you so, my dear girl,
Please forgive me,
For your brother's sake,
Forgive your mother
For your seventh birthday!

PRAYER

Oh, Lord!
You, who have made everything in this world,
You, who have given the breath of life to all,
You, in whom alone we place our trust,
Tell us: why?
A thousand times we have wondered
What is our, oh so grave, sin?
I know we have no right,
But we beseech You, help us!
You have given us the strength
To go on living,
Walking and working...
Give us the strength to have faith in You,
For the rest of our lives,
To follow Your path always.
Give us, o Lord, the strength to endure,
Help us to be righteous,
To deserve one day
Passage to your Love
And there to join
Our son.

COME BACK, MY SON

You were my everything,
My joy, my happiness,
My sorrow, my pain.
You were my pride, my trepidation,
You were everything to your mother.
Love of my heart,
My darkened future,
My unfulfilled desire,
My halted life.
My good and kind child,
My only son,
My tear, ever fresh,
Our desert-like home.
My brave and noble son,
Come back,
So we can start afresh,
Come back,
To end our sufferings.
Come back,
For we do know,
But refuse
To believe!

MOTHERS

Mothers can bear it when their children don't love them,
Mothers can bear it when their children leave them.
They can bear it when their children are ashamed of them,
They can even bear it when their children abandon them.
The only thing a mother cannot bear
Is to take white lilies
To her own child's grave.

THANK YOU

I thank you, my son,
For being full of love,
I thank you
For being such a good child.
I thank you, my son,
For being so helpful,
For bringing us solace,
For doing good at school.
I thank you
For having made us laugh,
I thank you also
For having made us cross.
I thank you
For the pride you made us feel,
I thank you
For those ten years of joy.
And I thank you, my son,
From the bottom of my heart,
For having had you.

RIVER

It runs and it flows,
That powerful river
Which once was
So clear and clean.
And the life bringing
Bicker was heard.
It runs and it flows,
On and on,
But it is either clear
Or clean no more.
It flows silently
Toward its mouth...
It would like to run back,
To return
To the place
Where it was once clear
And clean.
But there is no
Turning back!
It wallows silently,
Flowing towards its mouth.
A long time has passed
Since it was clear
Or clean.
It carries with it the mud
And the blood of heroes.
And it was once
So clear and clean.

IF ONLY!

If only I could have
That one moment of joy.
If only I could have
Some of that blue sky
And the song of birds!
If only I could have
That one moment of joy,
To see the brother
With his sister.
If I could only go back,
Just briefly, my God,
I would know how to appreciate
All the blessings sent my way!
When the sky was
Sacred and blue,
And smiles adorned
The faces of children.
Oh, if only,
If I could only
Kiss those eyes
That are no more!

THE CROSS

I carry my cross
And I stumble.
I fall under it,
But I get up.
Hills and valleys
Are behind me.
Gloom and void
Before me.

Anita Rakidžija was born in Dubrovnik in 1957. She works as an economist. When the war started she had to leave her home in Orašac and go with her children to Dubrovnik. As a refugee, she first finds shelter with relatives, and later in a hotel. After the occupying army has withdrawn from the wider Dubrovnik area she returns to Orašac with her family.

The hardships of war, her pain and suffering are described in this, her first book.

Anita Rakidžija